Campbell's
CLOCKWATCHERS
COOKBOOK

CLARE LATIMER

PRODUCED FOR CAMPBELL'S SOUPS
BY ESMONDE PUBLISHING AND VANDENBURG ASSOCIATES

Text © Clare Latimer, 1985

Published in Great Britain by
Esmonde Publishing Limited
8 The Talina Centre
Bagleys Lane
London SW6 2BW

© Esmonde Publishing Limited, 1985

© Campbell's Soups Limited, 1985

All rights reserved. No part of this publication may be reproduced or transmitted in any form or by any means, electronic or mechanical, including but not limited to photocopy, recording, or any information storage or retrieval system without prior permission from the publisher or copyright holder.

ISBN: 0 946680 10 8

Designed by Richard Kelly

Photography by Vernon Morgan

Phototypeset by Concise Graphics Limited
London W6 8NX

Printed by Nene Litho and bound by Woolnough Bookbinding
both of Irthlingborough, Northants

CONTENTS

Introduction	4
For Starters	5
For Fillers	25
For Daily Hits	49
For Globetrotters	77
For Well Being	99
For Parties	119
Index	139

INTRODUCTION

If you have ever wondered how you can cut down on time spent preparing meals but at the same time make your cooking more imaginative then Campbell's Condensed is for you. With its thick rich consistency, great natural taste and terrific range of flavours, Campbell's Condensed Soup is the clever cook's perfect shortcut to a new and exciting world of quick but impressive cookery.

Every recipe in the book is simple and quick to prepare – no endless list of ingredients or fancy equipment for Campbell's Clockwatchers. So if you are looking for new ideas to help you to relax and enjoy your party planning, to pep up family favourites or for interesting snacks and starters, you'll find it all here. We have given you over one hundred 'souper' recipes but we are sure that you are going to have lots of your own ideas. Try interchanging soups for new flavours. The combinations are endless so you can add to your repertoire and write down your good ideas in the space provided for Cook's Notes beneath each recipe.

EQUIPMENT   Don't worry if you don't have a food processor, liquidiser or blender, a bit of elbow grease and a hand-whisk will do the job equally well.

INGREDIENTS   All the ingredients, or optional ingredients, are easy to find. If you have to watch budgets as well as time then these recipes are ideal. Unless otherwise indicated, Campbell's Condensed Soups are to be added, undiluted, to the recipe.

HERBS   Don't worry if you cannot get fresh herbs, substitute with dried but use half the quantity.

PREPARATION TIME   Preparation time includes everything up to the moment the casserole is put in the oven or the lid is put on the saucepan.

COOKING AHEAD   Where suggestions are given for recipes which may be cooked in advance reheat these dishes gently to retain all the flavour. Most of the dishes in this book will take between 30 and 45 minutes in a moderate oven. Allow extra time if the food has been chilled or if you are using cast iron cookware.

FREEZING   Look for the (F) symbol indicating freezer storage time for dishes which may be frozen.

MICROWAVE   Look for the [M] symbol indicating cooking time where dishes may be cooked in the microwave. It may still be necessary to fry the ingredients but cooking time in the oven will be reduced. Don't use metal containers or foil in the microwave.

COOK'S NOTES   As a special feature we have provided space for you to write your own notes about the recipes. We suggest you try different soups from the wide range of Campbell's Condensed and note down your discoveries.

FOR STARTERS

With
Campbell's Condensed
you can whip up a mousse or
produce a pâté in just a few minutes.
Great news for today's Clockwatchers
who want to know the secret of
making interesting starters
in a hurry.

10 minutes
Preparation time

**Cooking time:
15 minutes**

Serves 4

Stuffed Mushrooms

A very nourishing and easy start to a meal. If you can't get the big flat mushrooms then use the cup ones. For a dinner party garnish the plate with salad items like radicchio, tomato and red pepper. A wedge of lemon and a leaf or two of lettuce make it look perfect for a family meal.

8 large flat mushrooms, wiped and stalks removed
a little oil
295 g (10.4 oz) Campbell's Condensed Crab Bisque
juice of ½ lemon
freshly ground black pepper
75 g (3 oz) Cheddar cheese, grated
Garnish: few lettuce leaves
1 lemon, cut into wedges

Preheat the oven, 180°C (350°F) or Gas 4. Oil a large baking tray and then lay on the mushrooms upside down. Brush each one with the oil. Mix the Crab Bisque, lemon and pepper together and spoon into each mushroom. Top with the cheese and put in the oven for 15 minutes or until the cheese is melting and bubbling.

Serve with chunks of warm granary bread.

(F)   2 months

[M]   2-3 minutes on high

Cook's notes:

Hot Avocado with Crab

Once tried it is hard to forget the lovely texture and taste of this quick and easy starter. If serving it at a dinner party top each one with soured cream and fresh dill.

4 ripe avocados
295 g (10.4 oz) Campbell's Condensed Crab Bisque
a dash of Tabasco
freshly ground black pepper
Garnish: 1 lemon cut into wedges

Preheat the oven, 180°C (350°F) or Gas 4. Cut each avocado in half and remove the stone. Cut the flesh into squares without damaging the skin. Scoop out with a spoon into an ovenproof dish and pour over the Crab Bisque seasoned with the Tabasco and pepper. Cover and heat in the oven for 15 minutes. Put back into the shells and garnish with the lemon wedges.

Serve with brown bread and butter.

[M] 2 minutes on high

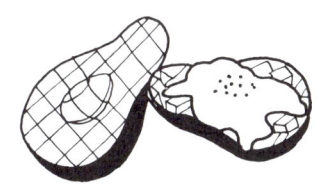

10 minutes
Preparation time

**Cooking time:
15 minutes**

Serves 8

Cook's notes:

FOR STARTERS · 7

15 *minutes*
Preparation time

**Chilling time:
1 hour**

Serves 8

Lamb's Liver Pâté

Simple to make and delicious to eat. The addition of apple gives a lovely fruity flavour without tasting too strong. It can be eaten with toast, used to stuff mushrooms, or spread in sandwiches with lettuce. Each way is irresistible.

50 g (2 oz) margarine
450 g (1 lb) lamb's liver
1 small cooking apple, peeled, cored and chopped
1 clove garlic, peeled and chopped
1 teasp sage
1 teasp thyme
2 tbsp sherry
295 g (10.4 oz) Campbell's Condensed French Onion Soup
freshly ground black pepper
50 g (2 oz) butter
1 tbsp chopped fresh parsley

Melt margarine in a frying pan and add the liver, apple, garlic, sage and thyme. Fry gently for 5 minutes. Add sherry, soup and pepper. Cook for a further 3 minutes. Blend or liquidize till smooth. Spoon into pâté dish and smooth over the top. Melt the butter, add the parsley and pour over the pâté making sure it covers the entire surface. Chill in the fridge for at least 1 hour.

Serve with piping hot toast.

(F)   2 months

Cook's notes:

Crowned Snaffles Mousse

This has to be one of Campbell's most famous recipes. The addition suggested here turns it into one of the smartest and most simple starters known.

295 g (10.4 oz) Campbell's Condensed Consomme
225 g (8 oz) packet Philadelphia cream cheese
1 pinch curry powder
1 clove garlic, peeled and roughly chopped
Garnish: 150 ml ($1/4$ pint) carton soured cream
1 small jar Danish lumpfish

Put the soup, cream cheese, curry powder and the garlic into a blender and whizz on maximum speed for 2 minutes. Pour into 6 small ramekin dishes and chill in the fridge for 2 hours. To serve, spoon a little soured cream on the top of each mousse and then top with a little lumpfish. Serve immediately.

Serve with thinly cut brown bread and butter.

5 minutes
Preparation time

Setting time:
2 hours

Serves 6

Cook's notes:

5 *minutes*
Preparation time

Serves 4

Chilled Consomme

A really quick and delicious starter or snack – so good that I always keep a can in the fridge.

295 g (10.4 oz) Campbell's Condensed Consomme, well chilled
150 ml (¼ pint) carton soured cream
1 small jar Danish lumpfish

When ready to serve spoon the Consomme into 4 glasses or ramekins. Spoon over the soured cream and top with a teaspoon of lumpfish. Serve immediately.

Serve with brown bread and butter.

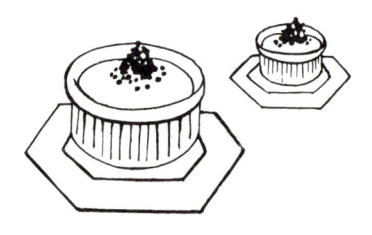

Cook's notes:

Anchovy and Onion Tart

This makes an excellent starter or a lovely surprise for a picnic.

225 g (8 oz) packet shortcrust pastry
295 g (10.4 oz) Campbell's Condensed French Onion Soup
3 eggs
1 tin anchovies
150 ml (¼ pint) milk or single cream
50 g (2 oz) Cheddar cheese, grated
freshly ground black pepper

Preheat the oven, 200°C (400°F) or Gas 6. Roll out and line a 23 cm (9 inch) quiche dish with the pastry, trim the edges, line with foil and fill with baking beans. Cook for 20 minutes and then remove foil and beans. Mix all the remaining ingredients together and pour into the pastry case. Cook in the oven for 20 minutes or until the mixture is set.

Serve with a salad.

Ⓕ   **3 months**

15 minutes
Preparation time

Cooking time: 40 minutes

Serves 4-6

Cook's notes:

FOR STARTERS · 11

15 minutes
Preparation time

Chilling time:
1 hour

Serves 6

Smoked Salmon Mousse in Lemon Shells

This is a very delicate dinner party starter; impressive in appearance and quick to make. You can either make double quantities to use up the soup and freeze the leftover mousse or use the rest of the can as soup. (The extra lemon juice can be kept in a bottle in the fridge for up to 2 weeks.)

6 large lemons
half of a 295 g (10.4 oz) Campbell's Condensed Cream of Smoked Salmon Soup
2 eggs, separated
freshly ground black pepper
1 tbsp mayonnaise
a dash of Tabasco
1 teasp gelatine
Garnish: fresh dill or parsley

Halve the lemons lengthways and carefully scoop out the flesh. Press out the juice into a bowl. Put the soup, egg yolks, black pepper, mayonnaise and Tabasco into another bowl and mix well. Put 1 tablespoon of lemon juice in a small saucepan and sprinkle over the gelatine. Leave for 1 minute. Place over a very low heat until dissolved. Pour into the soup mixture and stir well. Beat the egg whites until very stiff and then fold into the mixture. Spoon into the lemon shells and chill in the fridge for at least 1 hour. When ready to serve garnish with dill or parsley. Serve 2 per person.

Serve with thinly sliced brown bread and butter.

(F)   2 months

Cook's notes:

Asparagus Loaves

Asparagus loaves go beautifully with most starters or soups either served warm, straight from the oven, or toasted. If three loaves are too much you can easily freeze some of the mixture.
Make sure all the ingredients are at room temperature and you can't go wrong.

750 g (1½ lb) strong white flour
1 tbsp dried yeast
2 tbsp warm water
295 g (10.4 oz) Campbell's Condensed Asparagus Soup

Put the flour into a bowl. Mix the yeast and water together and leave to stand for 5 minutes. Pour into the flour mixture with the soup. Mix well into a pliable dough. Turn out onto a well floured surface and knead for 5 minutes. Grease 3 × 600 ml (1 pint) loaf tins. Divide the mixture into 3, shape and place in tins. Cover with a damp cloth and leave in a warm place for 1 hour. Preheat the oven, 200°C (400°F) or Gas 6. Bake in the oven for 30 minutes or until it sounds hollow when you tap the bottom of the loaf.

A great accompaniment to most starters.

Ⓕ   **2 months**

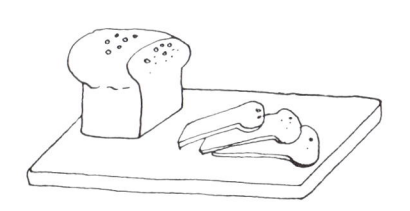

15 minutes
Preparation time

Rising time:
1 hour

Cooking time:
30 minutes

Makes 3 loaves

Cook's notes:

15 *minutes*
Preparation time

Setting time:
1 hour

Serves 8

Crab in Seashells

You can buy scallop shells at most fishmongers or even in seaside tourist shops. They are well worth using as they leave a perfect imprint on the mousse but you can also use small moulds or ramekins. If you have any mixture left over it can be poured into a bowl and served separately.

295 g (10.4 oz) Campbell's Condensed Crab Bisque
2 eggs, separated
freshly ground black pepper
a dash of Tabasco
juice of 1/2 lemon
25 g (1 oz) gelatine
150 ml (1/4 pint) double cream, lightly whipped
Garnish: 295 g (10.4 oz) Campbell's Condensed Asparagus Soup
1 pinch paprika
juice of 1/2 lemon
2 tbsp milk

Oil 8 scallop shells, small moulds or ramekins. Mix Crab Bisque, yolks, pepper and Tabasco together. Put lemon juice in small saucepan and sprinkle over gelatine. Leave 1 minute. Heat very slowly until dissolved and then add to the soup mixture. Stir in 4 tablespoons of cream. Whisk the egg whites and fold in. Carefully spoon the mixture into each shell. Leave to set in the fridge for 1 hour. To serve, mix the asparagus soup, the rest of the cream, paprika and lemon juice together. Pour on to 8 serving plates to cover the surface of each. Turn out 1 shell shape onto each plate. Sprinkle with paprika and serve.

Serve with asparagus tips.

(F)   2 months

Cook's notes:

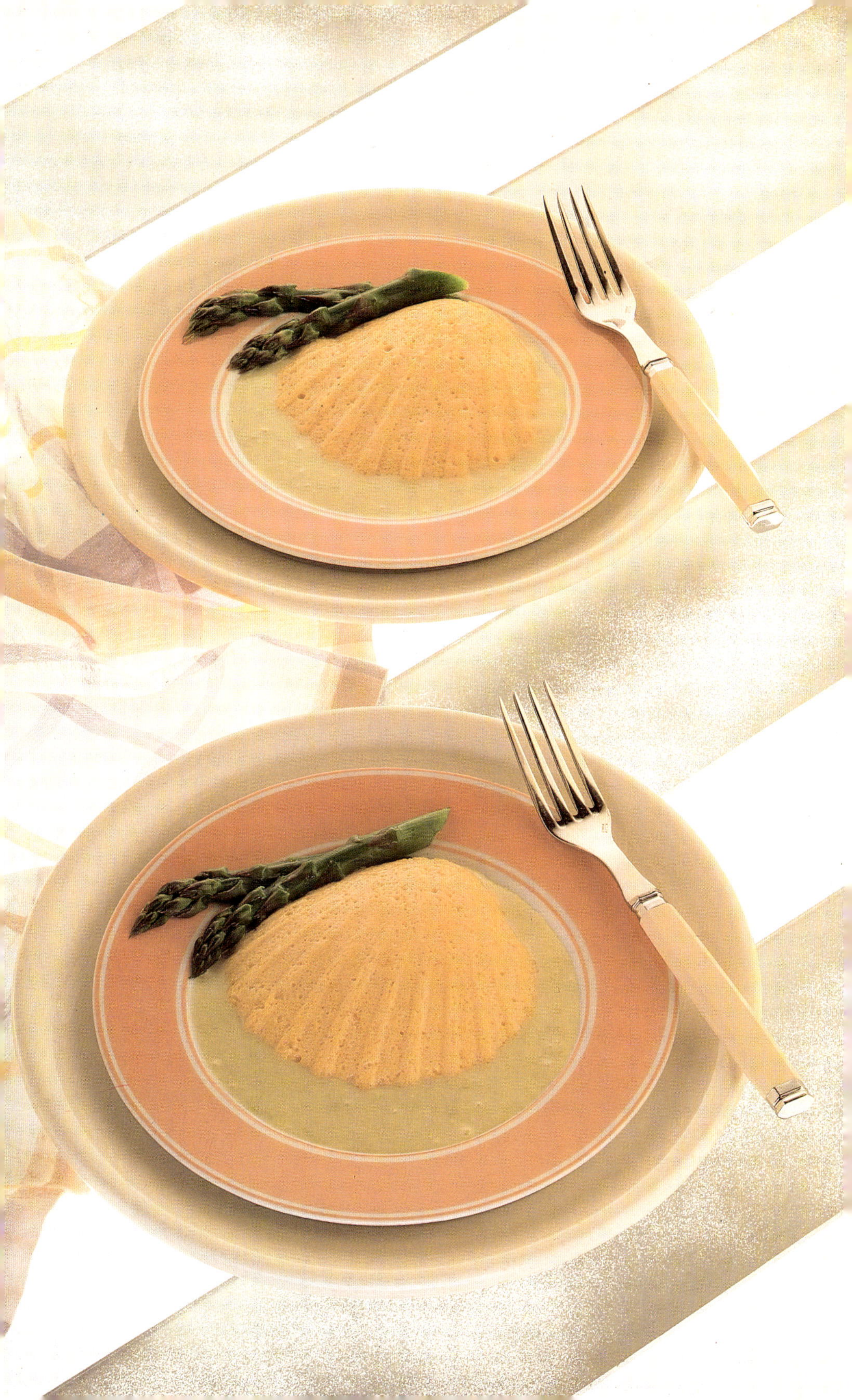

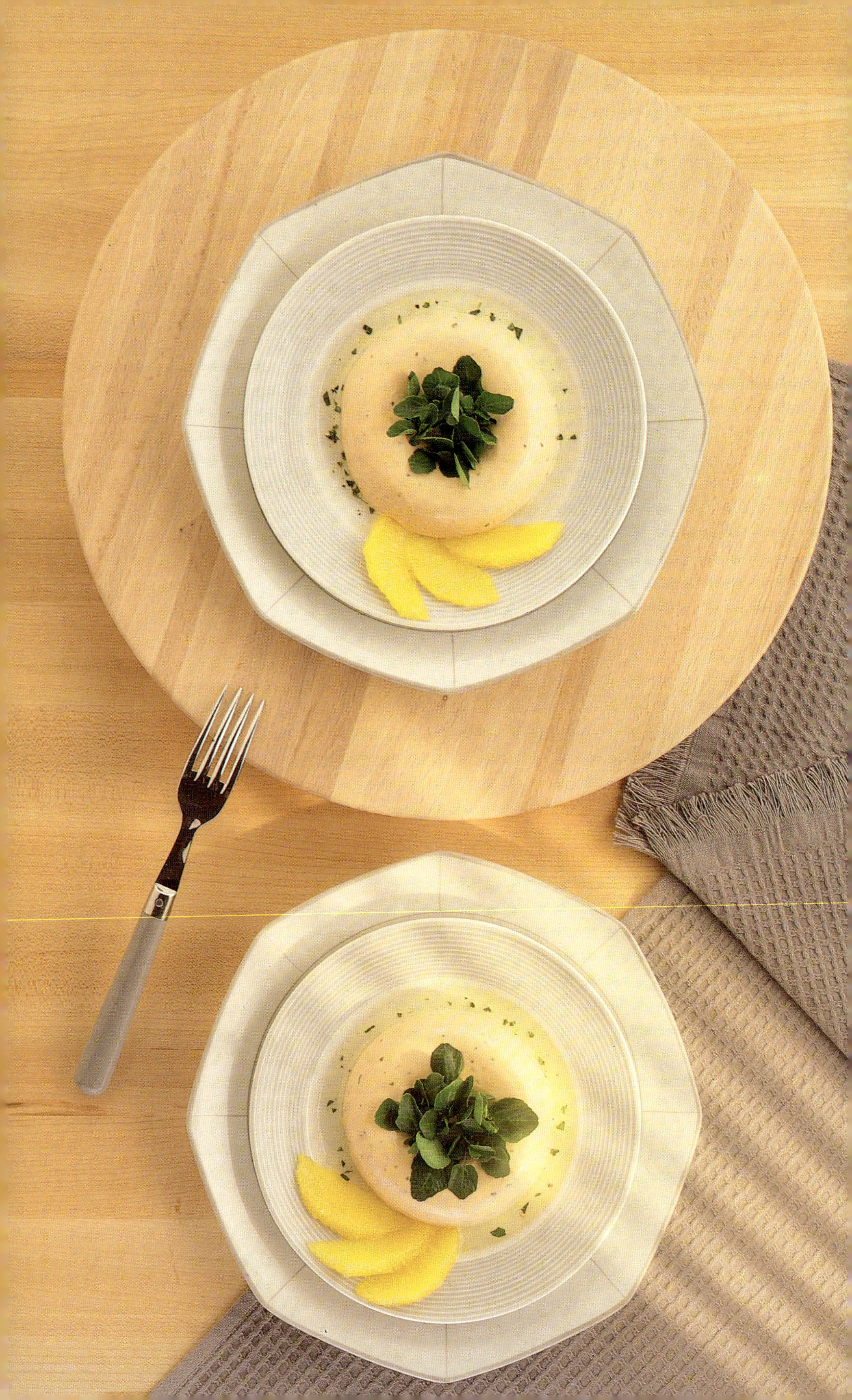

Tomato Moulds with Herb Sauce

Do not let horrors of turning out mousses deter you from trying this recipe. It takes seconds to prepare and once set in the fridge, it turns out with ease. If you are a real coward then serve it in a ramekin and garnish the top. Either way it is not to be missed!

300 g (10.6 oz) Campbell's Condensed Tomato Soup
150 ml (1/4 pint) orange juice
1 teasp basil
12 g (1/2 oz) gelatine
225 g (8 oz) Philadelphia cream cheese
150 ml (1/4 pint) carton soured cream

Herb Sauce
4 tbsp olive oil
1 tbsp chopped basil
a little salt and pepper
pinch of castor sugar
Garnish: watercress and orange segments

Oil 6 small moulds, 7 cm (2¾ inch), or 1 large 15 cm (6 inch) mould. Put the soup into a blender. Pour the orange juice into a small saucepan, sprinkle over the gelatine and the basil and then dissolve over low heat. Pour into the blender and add the cream cheese and soured cream. Blend on a high speed for 1 minute. Pour into 6 ramekins or small moulds, or one large mould, and chill in the fridge for 2 hours. Make up the herb sauce. When ready to serve, dip the moulds quickly into hot water up to the mousse level. Pour a little herb sauce onto each plate. Turn out the mousses and garnish.

Serve with brown bread and butter.

Ⓕ 2 months

---

15 minutes
Preparation time

**Setting time:
2 hours**

Serves 6

Cook's notes:

FOR STARTERS · 17

10 minutes
Preparation time

Setting time:
2 hours

Serves 4-6

Prawn and Herb Mousse

A very good light starter especially when served with a tomato and mushroom salad or dressed up with a few fresh herbs.

295 g (10.4 oz) Campbell's Condensed Consomme
225 g (8 oz) Boursin cheese
50 g (2 oz) peeled prawns
Garnish: extra prawns and parsley

Put ¾ of the can of soup into a blender with the cheese and whizz well. Stir in the prawns (reserve 4 for garnish) and pour the mixture into 4 ramekins or glasses. Leave to set in the fridge. When firm pour the rest of the soup over the 4 dishes and again chill in the fridge until the top is set. Garnish with prawns and little sprigs of parsley.

Serve with triangles of toast.

Cook's notes:

Seafood Shells

These look attractive served in china shell dishes, scallop shells or ramekins.

450 g (l lb) fresh crab meat
295 g (10.4 oz) Campbell's Condensed Cream of Smoked Salmon Soup
juice of 1 lemon
freshly ground black pepper
a dash of Tabasco
2 tbsp breadcrumbs
25 g (1 oz) Cheddar cheese, grated
Garnish: fresh dill or parsley, wedges of lemon and lettuce leaves

Mix the crab, soup, lemon juice, pepper and Tabasco together in a bowl. Spoon into shells or ramekins. Sprinkle over the breadcrumbs mixed with the cheese. Place under a medium hot grill. Watch carefully for about 8-10 minutes or until bubbling and turning golden in colour. Garnish with fresh herbs, lemon and lettuce leaves.

10 minutes
Preparation time

Cooking time:
10 minutes

Serves 8

Cook's notes:

10 minutes
Preparation time

Setting time:
1 hour

Serves 4

Cream Ham Mousse

This could be a starter for a dinner party or a summer main course served with a selection of salads. It is very quick to make and can be left in the fridge to set while you cook the rest of the meal.

350 g (12 oz) cooked ham, sliced or chopped
295 g (10.4 oz) Campbell's Condensed Consomme
1 tbsp brandy
1 teasp French mustard
1 teasp Worcestershire sauce
a dash of Tabasco
150 ml (¼ pint) double cream, lightly whipped
Garnish: sprigs of watercress and cucumber slices

Put the ham and consomme into the blender and turn on maximum speed for 1 minute or until the mixture is smooth. Pour into a large bowl and stir in the brandy, Worcestershire sauce, mustard and Tabasco. Fold in the cream and then put into a serving dish. Leave to set in the fridge and then garnish with the watercress and slices of cucumber.

Serve with crusty rolls.

Cook's notes:

Stuffed Eggs with Asparagus

A very simple dish, perfect for a summertime lunch or as a light meal. You can prepare it in advance and just pipe in the filling before serving.

10 minutes
Preparation time

Serves 6

6 hard-boiled eggs, shelled
half a can of 295 g (10.4 oz) Campbell's Condensed Asparagus Soup
1 tbsp mayonnaise
freshly ground black pepper
a little lemon juice
Garnish: few lettuce leaves, paprika

Cut eggs in half lengthways. Remove the yolks, taking care not to break the whites. Wash and drain the whites. Cream together the yolks, soup, mayonnaise, pepper and lemon juice. Put into a piping bag and pipe into the egg whites. Arrange on a serving dish with the lettuce leaves and sprinkle with paprika.

Serve with a mixed salad.

Cook's notes:

10 minutes
Preparation time

Setting time:
1-2 hours

Serves 4

Consommed Eggs

A popular starter made extra special if topped with soured cream and a spoonful of Danish lumpfish (roe).

4 hard-boiled eggs, shelled and sliced
295 g (10.4 oz) Campbell's Condensed Consomme
2 tbsp sherry
1 teasp freshly chopped basil

Place an egg in each ramekin dish. Put the consomme, sherry and basil into a saucepan and heat slightly. Pour over the eggs and leave to set in the fridge for at least 1 hour. Serve straight from the fridge.

Serve with hot toast.

Cook's notes:

Layered Fish Terrine

This is the king of all terrines using three different Campbell's soups to cut preparation time to a minimum. Any chef would be proud of the result.

Bottom Layer
225 g (8 oz) smoked haddock, cooked, boned and skinned
1 tbsp mayonnaise
1 level dessertsp gelatine
150 ml (¼ pint) double cream, lightly whipped
1 tbsp parsley, chopped

Middle Layer
225 g (8 oz) cod fillet, cooked and skinned
156 g (5½ oz) Campbell's Condensed Cream of Celery Soup
juice ½ lemon
1 level dessertsp gelatine

Top Layer
295 g (10.4 oz) Campbell's Condensed Cream of Smoked Salmon Soup
1 egg, separated
juice of ½ lemon
2 level dessertsp gelatine

30 *minutes*
Preparation time

Setting time:
5 hours or overnight

Serves 8 from each terrine

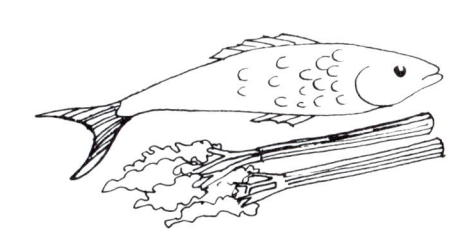

continued overleaf

Oil 2 × 600 ml (1 pint) loaf tins. To make bottom layer, mix the smoked haddock and mayonnaise well. Put lemon juice in small saucepan, sprinkle over gelatine, soak and then dissolve over very low heat. Add cream and parsley to the mixture. Put half the mixture into each tin and chill. For second layer, mix fish and celery soup together, repeat gelatine method and mix well. Put over haddock layer and chill again. For the top layer, put the smoked salmon soup into a bowl with the egg yolk. Repeat the gelatine method. Add to soup and fold in well beaten egg white. Pour into tins, cover and chill well overnight.

Tomato Sauce
300 g (10.6 oz) Campbell's Condensed Cream of Tomato Soup
4 tbsp water
1 teasp basil, chopped

To serve: mix sauce well and cover the surface of each plate. Turn out terrine, slice and arrange on the sauce.

Ⓕ   2 months (terrine only)

Cook's notes:

FOR FILLERS

A hectic life style often means you don't have time to stop for proper meals, so use Campbell's Condensed for a 'souper' filler at any time of the day. And there are lots of other snacks which are as quick to prepare as a sandwich, but much more exciting. Great ideas too for quick lunches or for picnics.

15 minutes
Preparation time

**Cooking time:
15 minutes**

Serves 4

Porky Pea Soup

A lovely warming soup which only takes minutes to make and certainly does the trick on a wintry day.

125 g (4 oz) streaky bacon, derinded and chopped, OR 1 tbsp oil
1 onion, peeled and finely chopped
1 stalk celery, washed and finely chopped
295 g (10.4 oz) Campbell's Condensed Pea and Ham Soup
300 ml (½ pint) water
2 frankfurters, thinly sliced
Garnish: 1 tbsp double cream, 1 dessertsp chopped parsley

Put the bacon or oil, onion and celery in a saucepan over a low heat and cook for about 3 minutes. Add the soup and water and stir well. Bring to the boil and then simmer for 15 minutes. Add frankfurters, stir well and then serve. Garnish each bowl with cream and parsley.

Serve with chunks of warm granary bread.

Ⓕ   1 month

Cook's notes:

Vichyssoise

This is a wonderful summer soup that can be made in advance and then well chilled in the fridge. A soup to produce on a hot day to cool you down and fill you up.

15 minutes
Preparation time

Cooking time:
10 minutes

Chilling time:
1 hour

Serves 4

1 large potato, peeled and finely chopped
8 spring onions, washed and chopped
600 ml (1 pint) water
295 g (10.4 oz) Campbell's Condensed Cream of Chicken Soup
freshly ground black pepper
150 ml (¼ pint) soured cream
Garnish: 1 tbsp chopped chives, a little grated nutmeg

Boil the potato and spring onions in the water for 10 minutes. Liquidize. Add the soup and pepper and stir well. Chill for 1 hour or more. Stir in the soured cream and pour into soup bowls. Sprinkle over the chives and nutmeg and serve.

Serve with brown bread and butter.

Cook's notes:

5 *minutes*
Preparation time

**Cooking time:
5 minutes**

Serves 4

Curried Sweetcorn Soup

Chicken and sweetcorn have always been a good combination and the gentle hint of curry makes this soup near perfection.

295 g (10.4 oz) Campbell's Condensed Cream of Chicken Soup
300 ml (½ pint) water
¼ teasp curry paste
198 g (7 oz) can sweetcorn, creamed or plain
freshly ground black pepper
a little ground coriander
150 ml (¼ pint) single cream
Garnish: a little paprika

Put the soup and water into a saucepan. Stir well. Add the curry paste, corn, pepper and the coriander. Bring to the boil. Simmer for 5 minutes stirring frequently and then add the cream. Serve in soup bowls and garnish with paprika.

Serve with hot herb or garlic bread.

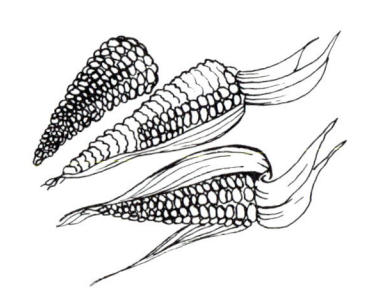

Cook's notes:

Floating Crab Soup

Here you have the easiest soup in the world to make but, more important, the most impressive. Floating on the top of the soup are puff pastry crab shapes with a surprise filling of soured cream. Store extra crab shapes in a tin.

15 *minutes*
Preparation time

Cooking time:
10 minutes

Serves 4

295 g (10.4 oz) Campbell's Condensed Crab Bisque
juice of ½ lemon
freshly ground black pepper
2 tbsp dry sherry
300 ml (½ pint) milk
225 g (8 oz) packet frozen or fresh puff pastry, well chilled
1 egg, beaten
150 ml (¼ pint) soured cream

Preheat the oven, 200°C (400°F) or Gas 6. Put the soup, lemon, pepper, sherry and milk in a saucepan and heat very slowly. Roll out pastry on a floured board and, using a very sharp knife, cut out some crab shapes. The crabs should be about 7 cm (3 inches) in length. Lay on a baking tray, brush with the beaten egg and cook for 10 minutes or until golden brown. Leave to cool for a few minutes and then, using a teaspoon handle, scoop out the soft pastry by making a small hole underneath each crab and fill with soured cream. Bring the soup to boiling point and pour into 4 soup bowls; top each with a stuffed crab and serve.

crab shape in pastry

Cook's notes:

15 *minutes*
Preparation time

**Cooking time:
15 minutes**

Serves 4-6

Cartwheel Soup

Perfect soup for those watching their waistline. Fresh vegetables cooked in a clear consomme with a sprinkling of pasta. Also a good light starter to precede a rich main course.

Small bunch watercress, stalks removed and finely chopped
1 carrot, peeled and diced very small
1 stalk celery, washed and diced very small
1 leek, washed and finely chopped
295 g (10.4 oz) Campbell's Condensed Consomme
300 ml (½ pint) water
25 g (1 oz) cartwheel-shaped pasta
freshly ground black pepper
2 tbsp dry sherry
Garnish: finely chopped parsley

Put the prepared vegetables in a large saucepan with the soup and water and bring to the boil. Reduce heat. Cover and simmer for 5 minutes. Add the pasta and cover and cook for a further 8 minutes. Add the pepper and sherry and pour into soup bowls. Garnish with the chopped parsley and serve.

Cook's notes:

Smoked Mackerel Pâté

Smoked mackerel is always popular. This pâté is an excellent snack with toast or in sandwiches. The horseradish gives it a really good tang.

10 minutes
Preparation time

Serves 4-6

225 g (8 oz) smoked mackerel, skinned and boned
juice of ½ lemon
freshly ground black pepper
1 teasp horseradish sauce
156 g (5½ oz) Campbell's Condensed Cream of Celery Soup
Garnish: slices of radish and a few lemon wedges

Blend all the ingredients in a liquidizer or beat well in a bowl. Put into a pâté dish and garnish with radish slices and lemon wedges.

Serve with hot toast.

Ⓕ   1 month

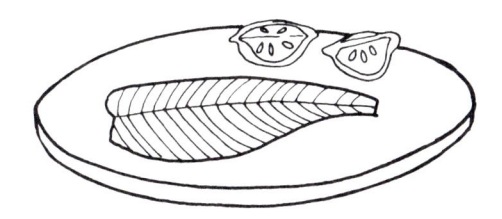

Cook's notes:

15 minutes
Preparation time

**Cooking time:
15 minutes**

Serves 8

Bouillabaisse

Bouillabaisse provides a great opportunity to combine all kinds of fresh or frozen fish to make a feast from the sea.

1 tbsp oil
1 medium onion, peeled and chopped
3 cloves garlic, peeled and crushed
1 teasp turmeric or saffron
1 medium-sized leek, cut into slices and washed well
mixed spoonful parsley, thyme and bayleaves
300 g (10.6 oz) Campbell's Condensed Cream of Tomato Soup
295 g (10.4 oz) Campbell's Condensed Crab Bisque
150 ml (¼ pint) white wine
300 ml (½ pint) water
peel from one orange (optional)
freshly ground black pepper
225 g (8 oz) thickly cut cod
225 g (8 oz) thickly cut halibut
225 g (8 oz) monkfish tail, on the bone
150 ml (¼ pint) mussels in the shell
150 ml (¼ pint) prawns in the shell
6 crab or lobster claws
juice of 1 lemon

Put the oil in a large saucepan. Add the onion, garlic, turmeric, leek and herbs and fry gently for about 3 minutes. Then add all the other ingredients, stir gently, cover and bring to the boil. Simmer for 15 minutes and serve in soup bowls. The shells add great flavour but are not meant to be eaten!

Serve with chunks of garlic or herb bread.

Cook's notes:

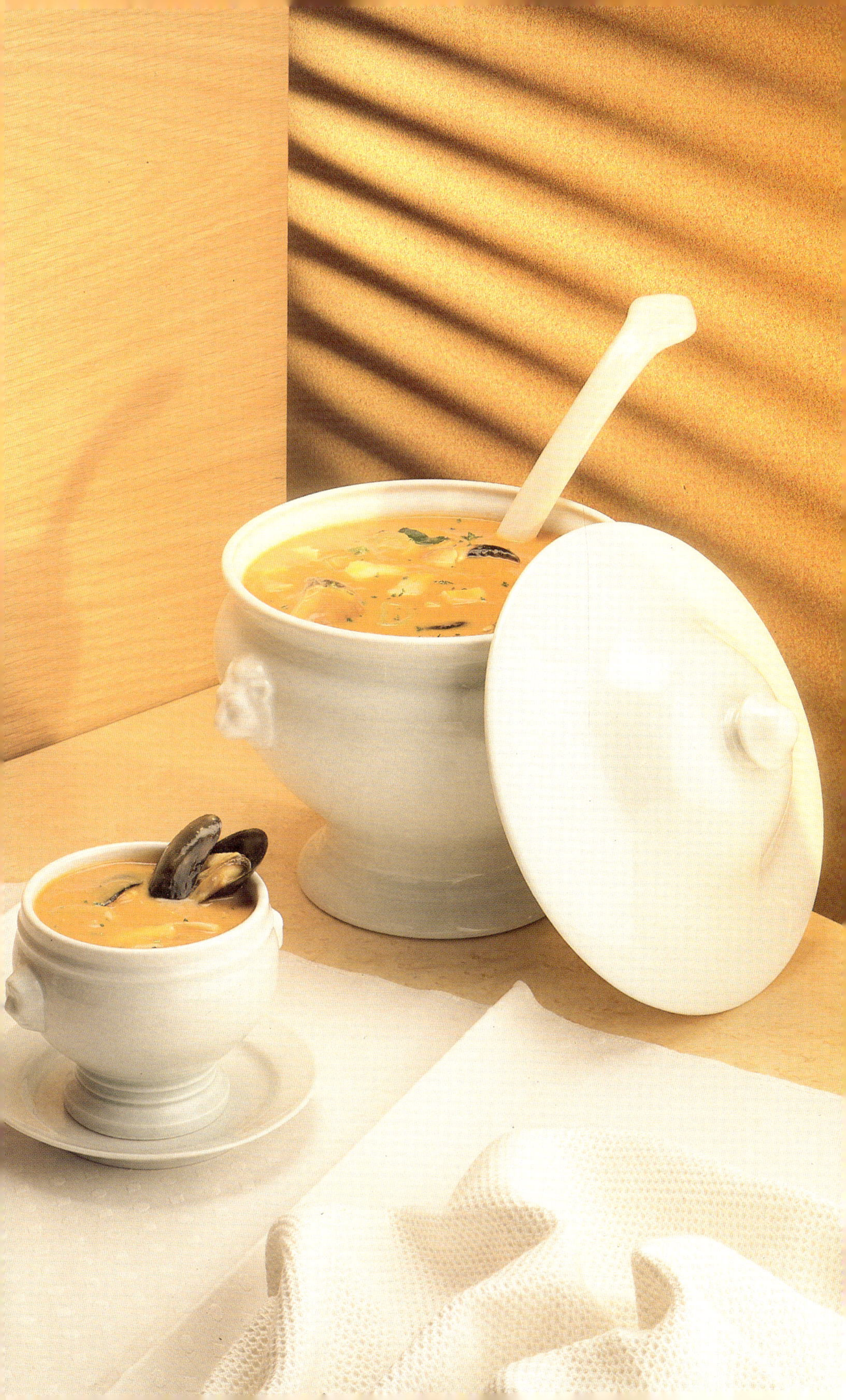

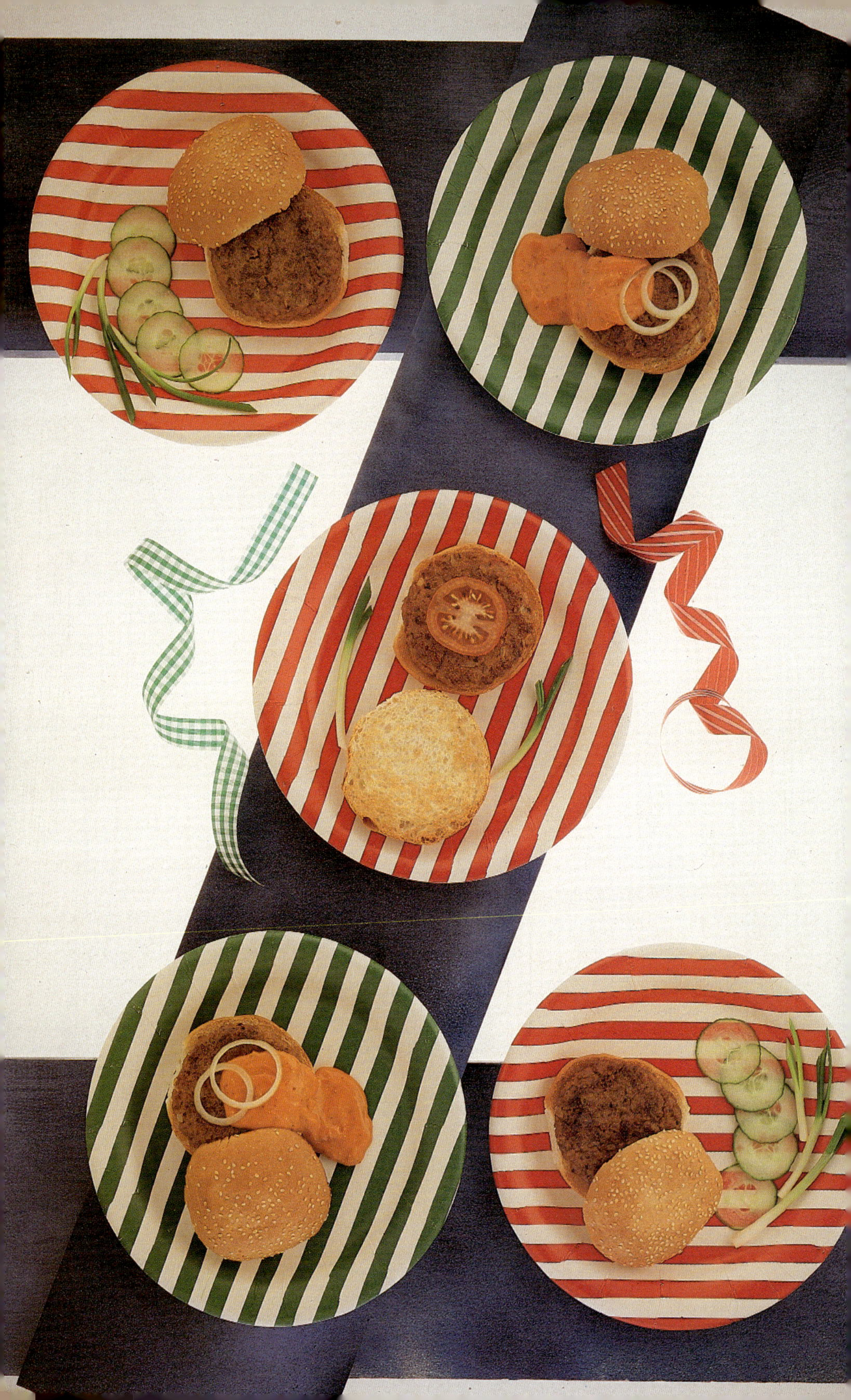

Spicy Hamburgers

A children's favourite but secretly enjoyed by adults too.

15 minutes Preparation time

Cooking time: 10 minutes

Serves 4-6

Hamburgers
1 onion, peeled and finely chopped
450 g (1 lb) lean mince
75 g (3 oz) fine breadcrumbs
1 teasp oregano
300 g (10.6 oz) Campbell's Condensed Cream of Tomato Soup
1 egg
freshly ground black pepper

Sauce
1 teasp Worcestershire sauce
a dash of Tabasco
1 teasp seed mustard
a little lemon or orange juice
remaining half can of Campbell's Condensed Cream of Tomato Soup

Mix all the hamburger ingredients together *using half the soup only*. Roll out 6-8 balls and then flatten. Grill or fry each for 10 minutes turning once. Meanwhile, mix all the sauce ingredients together and put into a serving bowl.

Serve in baps with the sauce and a salad or on their own with cottage cheese and a green salad.

(F) freeze raw up to 2 months

[M] 5-7 minutes on high

Cook's notes:

10 *minutes*
Preparation time

Serves 6

Prawn and Cheese Pâté

This is a lovely fresh and crunchy pâté that can be served with biscuits for cocktails or as a snack with hot toast.

350 g (12 oz) cream cheese
juice of ½ lemon
156 g (5½ oz) Campbell's Condensed Cream of Celery Soup
1 small onion, peeled and finely chopped
freshly ground black pepper
125 g (4 oz) frozen prawns, thawed and dried
Garnish: watercress

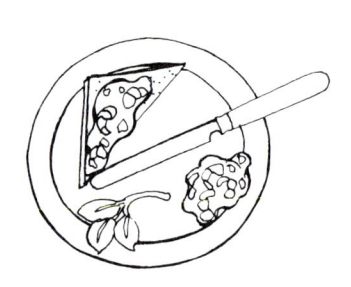

Blend the cream cheese, lemon juice and soup together until smooth. Stir in the onion, pepper and prawns and mix well. Place in a pâté dish and garnish with a few sprigs of watercress.

Serve with hot toast.

Cook's notes:

Cheese and Celery Scones

These cheese and celery scones are ideal with soup. Remember to make scones with a very light hand and this will keep them airy.

225 g (8 oz) self-raising flour
¼ teasp dried mustard
50 g (2 oz) margarine
50 g (2 oz) Cheddar cheese, finely grated
156 g (5½ oz) Campbell's Condensed Cream of Celery Soup
4 tbsp water
a little milk

Preheat the oven, 220°C (425°F) or Gas 7. Sift the flour and mustard into a bowl. Add fat and rub in until the mixture resembles breadcrumbs. Stir in the cheese. Beat the soup and water together and add to the mixture making a soft dough. Turn dough onto a floured surface and knead very lightly. Roll out dough lightly to 2 cm (1 inch) thickness and cut out scones using a pastry cutter. Place on a baking tray and brush with milk. Bake in the oven for 20 minutes or until light brown on top. Serve warm.

(F)   3 months

15 minutes
Preparation time

Cooking time: 20 minutes

Serves 8-10

Cook's notes:

15 minutes
Preparation time

Cooking time:
8-15 minutes

Vol au Vents

These make excellent quick snacks and all the ingredients are normally to hand. Use small cocktail vol au vents to serve with drinks, the medium ones for starters and the large ones for snacks or main courses.

To cook vol au vents
Preheat the oven, 200°C (400°F) or Gas 6. Use frozen vol au vents, lay on a baking tray and brush the top of each with beaten egg. Cook for 8-15 minutes depending on the size. Leave to cool and then using a sharp knife, cut out the centres at the top. Keep 'lids' to put back after you have filled each one.

Various filling ideas
Campbell's Condensed Cream of Chicken Soup with small can sweetcorn
Campbell's Condensed Cream of Mushroom Soup with Worcestershire sauce
Campbell's Condensed Cream of Celery Soup with sliced ham finely chopped
Campbell's Condensed Crab Bisque with chopped hard-boiled egg
Campbell's Condensed Cream of Smoked Salmon with lemon juice and soured cream
Campbell's Condensed Asparagus Soup with lemon juice and yoghurt

Each filling should be sufficient for approximately 30 small vol au vents, 12 medium or 6 large.

[M]　3 minutes on high for filling

Cook's notes:

Baked Potatoes with various fillings

10 minutes
Preparation time

Cooking time:
30 minutes-
1 hour

Serves 8

Baked potatoes are a very popular snack. To prepare the potatoes: wash each potato well and prick with a knife to prevent it from bursting. Rub each potato in oil and salt. Preheat the oven, 200°C (400°F) or Gas 6. Bake for at least 30 minutes to 1 hour depending on the size of the potato. To speed cooking time put the potatoes on a metal skewer or baked potato stand. Cut a cross into the top of each potato and ease apart the four quarters to make an opening.
Blend the cooked potato with these fillings:

1. Celery and Cheese
295 g (10.4 oz) Campbell's Condensed Cream of Celery Soup
1/4 teasp paprika
50 g (2 oz) Cheddar cheese, grated
a little mustard
freshly ground black pepper
a little milk

Mix all together and spoon into the open potatoes. Will fill 4 potatoes.

2. Mushroom Spiked filling
295 g (10.4 oz) Campbell's Condensed Cream of Mushroom Soup
150 ml (1/4 pint) soured cream
1/2 teasp Worcestershire sauce

Mix all together and spoon into the open potatoes. Will fill 4 potatoes.

[M] 5 minutes on high for potatoes
[M] 1 minute on high for filling

Cook's notes:

10 minutes
Preparation time

Cooking time:
3-5 minutes

Serves 4-8

Catalonian Bread

This is a kind of toasted bread with the superb flavours of tomato, garlic and herbs all cooked together until perfectly blended. It is excellent with soup.

8 slices bread
a little butter
1 clove garlic, peeled and crushed
156 g (5½ oz) Campbell's Condensed Cream of Tomato Soup
25 g (1 oz) Cheddar cheese, grated
1 teasp basil, preferably fresh, chopped

Toast the bread on one side under the grill. Spread with butter on the untoasted side. Mix all the rest of the ingredients together and then spread on the toast. Put under hot grill for about 3-5 minutes or until bubbling and turning golden brown. Cut into triangles and serve with bowls of soup.

(F) 2 months

Cook's notes:

Chicory and Ham Beds

Quick and easy and one of my old favourites. Use chicory, celery or leeks, canned or fresh.

2 good-sized pieces chicory
4 slices ham
a little butter
295 g (10.4 oz) Campbell's Condensed Asparagus Soup
juice of ½ lemon
2 tbsp double cream, lightly whipped (optional)
50 g (2 oz) grated Cheddar cheese

Preheat the oven, 200°C (400°F) or Gas 6. Cook the fresh chicory, celery or leeks in boiling salted water for 10 minutes. Drain and cut each one in half lengthways. Wrap each piece with the ham slices and place in a buttered ovenproof dish. Mix the soup, lemon juice and cream in a bowl and pour over the chicory and ham. Sprinkle the cheese over the top and bake in the oven for 15 minutes or until golden brown and bubbling.

Serve with baked or new potatoes.

15 minutes
Preparation time

Cooking time:
25 minutes

Serves 2

Cook's notes:

10 minutes
Preparation time

Cooking time:
20 minutes

Serves 6

Devilled Grilled Eggs

A perfect lunch snack and very quick and easy to make. You can prepare it the night before and heat it up before serving. Just right on a hectic day.

6 hard-boiled eggs, shelled and chopped
125 g (4 oz) prawns, chopped
295 g (10.4 oz) Campbell's Condensed Cream of Chicken Soup
2 tbsp milk
125 g (4 oz) Cheddar cheese, grated
1 tbsp breadcrumbs
1 teasp curry powder

Preheat the oven, 200°C (400°F) or Gas 6. Divide the eggs and prawns between 6 ramekin dishes. Mix together the soup, milk and half the cheese. Spoon over the eggs. Combine the rest of the cheese with the breadcrumbs and curry powder and sprinkle over each ramekin. Stand dishes on a baking tray and cook in the oven for 20 minutes or until bubbling and the cheese has melted.

Serve with bread and butter.

[M]   3 minutes on high

Cook's notes:

Pizza Baps

These are easy to make as the base is ready to use which saves going to the trouble of making dough.

15 minutes
Preparation time

**Cooking time:
20 minutes**

Makes 12 pizzas

6 large baps
2 tbsp olive oil
1 onion, peeled and chopped
50 g (2 oz) button mushrooms, wiped and sliced
300 g (10.6 oz) Campbell's Condensed Cream of Tomato Soup
freshly ground black pepper
1 teasp basil
12 anchovies halved lengthways
125 g (4 oz) Mozzarella or Cheddar cheese
12 black olives

Preheat the oven, 180°C (350°F) or Gas 4. Cut each bap in half and brush the insides with oil. Fry the onion and mushrooms for 3 minutes in the rest of the oil. Spread a little tomato soup on each bap surface, top each with the onion mixture and then some more tomato soup. Sprinkle over the pepper and basil and then arrange the anchovies in a star on top. Top with a layer of cheese and place an olive on top of each bap half. Place on a baking tray and cook for 20 minutes.

(F)   2 months

Cook's notes:

FOR FILLERS · 43

10 minutes
Preparation time

**Cooking time:
20 minutes**

Serves 2

Tuna Florentine

Very simple and full of goodness. If you wish you can use fresh fish or chicken instead of the tuna.

225 g (8 oz) packet frozen spinach, thawed
198 g (7 oz) can tuna
156 g (5½ oz) Campbell's Condensed Cream of Chicken Soup
3 tbsp milk
125 g (4 oz) Cheddar cheese, grated
Garnish: 2 tomatoes, cut into wedges

Preheat the oven, 190°C (375°F) or Gas 5. Drain liquid from spinach and place in a greased ovenproof dish. Drain oil from tuna, break up and arrange on the spinach. Whisk soup with milk and cheese and pour over the tuna. Bake in the oven for 20 minutes or until golden brown on top.

Serve with a crisp green salad.

M 6 minutes on high

Cook's notes:

44 · FOR FILLERS

Seafood Tart

A more unusual snack but still very quick and easy, particularly if you have a ready-made pastry case. Very good for a picnic.

225 g (8 oz) shortcrust pastry
3 eggs
295 g (10.4 oz) Campbell's Condensed Cream of Smoked Salmon Soup
150 ml (¼ pint) milk or cream
125 g (4 oz) frozen prawns, thawed and drained
freshly ground black pepper
a dash of Tabasco
juice of ½ lemon
1 tbsp chopped parsley
50 g (2 oz) Cheddar cheese

Preheat the oven, 180°C (350°F) or Gas 4. Roll out the pastry to fit 23 cm (9 inch) quiche dish. Cover with foil and fill with baking beans and bake in oven for 20 minutes. Meanwhile, mix all remaining ingredients together and after removing the foil and baking beans pour into the pastry case. Cook for 25 minutes or until set.

Serve with an iceberg lettuce and cucumber salad.

(F) 2 months, but use fresh prawns

**15 minutes
Preparation time**

**Cooking time:
45 minutes**

Serves 4-6

Cook's notes:

10 *minutes*
Preparation time

Cooking time:
35 minutes

Serves 4

Macaroni Chicken

An old favourite, reminiscent of childhood. A good, nourishing and economical snack with a meaty flavour.

225 g (8 oz) macaroni
salt and freshly ground black pepper
125 g (4 oz) ham, cooked and diced
3 large tomatoes, skinned and chopped
295 g (10.4 oz) Campbell's Condensed Cream of Chicken Soup
50 g (2 oz) Cheddar cheese, grated

Preheat the oven, 200°C (400°F) or Gas 6. Cook the macaroni in boiling salted water for about 15 minutes or until just tender and then drain. Mix the remaining ingredients together and then stir in the macaroni using a wooden spoon. Pour into a buttered ovenproof dish and bake in the oven for 20 minutes or until the top is golden brown.

Serve with a mixed salad.

Ⓕ   2 months

Cook's notes:

Scrambled Egg with Chicken

This is very quick and easy and makes a lovely change from plain scrambled egg.

156 g (5½ oz) Campbell's Condensed Cream of Chicken Soup
4 eggs
freshly ground black pepper
25 g (1 oz) margarine

Place all the ingredients in a small non-stick saucepan and put over a low heat. Stir continuously with a wooden spoon until the mixture thickens and turns creamy. Serve immediately.

Serve with hot toast and a tomato salad.

5 minutes
Preparation time

Cooking time:
5 minutes

Serves 2-3

Cook's notes:

10 minutes
Preparation time

Cooking time:
20 minutes

Serves 2

Spinach Bed for Eggs

Popeye would have been glad of this recipe to vary his intake of spinach but Popeye or no Popeye this dish is pretty addictive. It is very quick to prepare and if you want to make it really different, add a handful of pine kernels to the spinach mixture.

225 g (8 oz) packet frozen spinach
295 g (10.4 oz) Campbell's Condensed Cream of Chicken Soup
freshly grated nutmeg
a little butter
4 small eggs
grated Parmesan cheese

Preheat the oven, 200°C (400°F) or Gas 6. Cook the spinach according to the packet instructions and drain very well. Mix with the chicken soup and nutmeg. Put into a buttered ovenproof dish, smooth over and, using the back of a serving spoon, press four indents into the surface. Crack one egg into each indent, sprinkle with salt and pepper and then bake in the oven for 10 minutes (vary the time depending on how you like your egg cooked). Sprinkle with Parmesan and serve.

Serve with chunks of granary bread and butter.

Cook's notes:

FOR DAILY HITS

Campbell's Condensed can really help Clockwatchers cut down on preparation time and pep up everyday family favourites. This collection of recipes will help you score number one hits every time.

20 minutes
Preparation time

Cooking time: 25 minutes

Serves 4-6

Chicken and Banana Pie

Here is a delicious chicken pie full of surprises such as red pepper, sausages, bacon and even bananas. You can't deep freeze this dish with the bananas as they turn black, but you can freeze it with oranges.

1 medium-sized cooked chicken, boned and chopped into cubes
295 g (10.4 oz) Campbell's Condensed Celery Soup
3 tbsp milk
2 herb sausages, grilled and chopped
3 rashers bacon, grilled and chopped
125 g (4 oz) sweetcorn
1 red pepper, cored and chopped
1 large banana, skinned and sliced or 2 oranges, sliced
225 g (8 oz) shortcrust pastry
1 tbsp parsley
freshly ground black pepper
1 egg, beaten

Preheat the oven, 200°C (400°F) or Gas 6. Roll out the pastry to cover a 1 litre (2 pint) pie dish. Mix all the remaining ingredients together in a saucepan and heat gently. Pour in the chicken mixture, wet the edges of the dish with water and then lay on the pastry. Press down well and trim the edges with a sharp knife. To seal, press down all round with a fork. Brush with the beaten egg and bake in the oven for 25 minutes or until the pastry is golden brown.

Serve with green beans and perhaps a baked potato for the hungry.

(F) 2 months (with oranges)

Cook's notes:

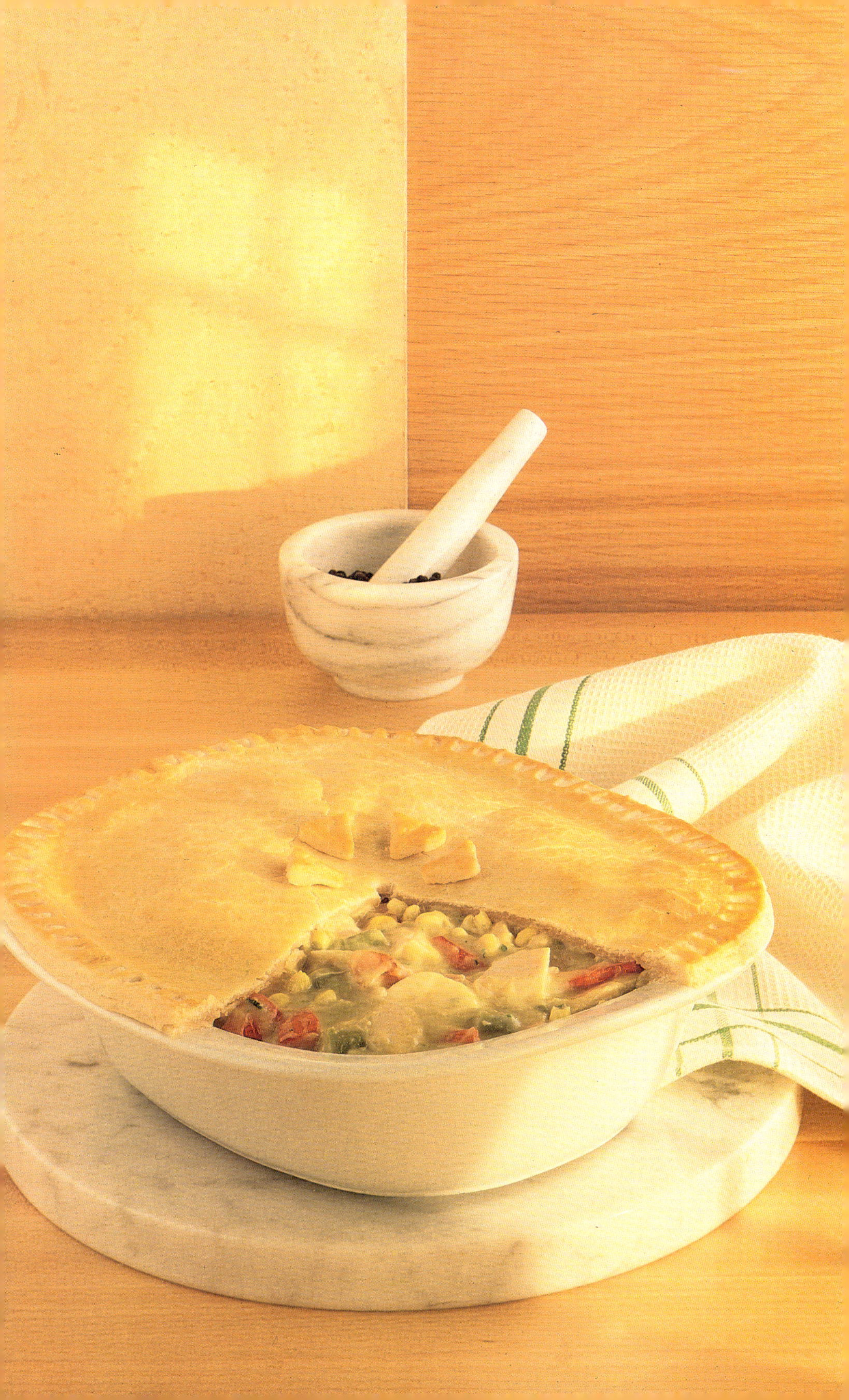

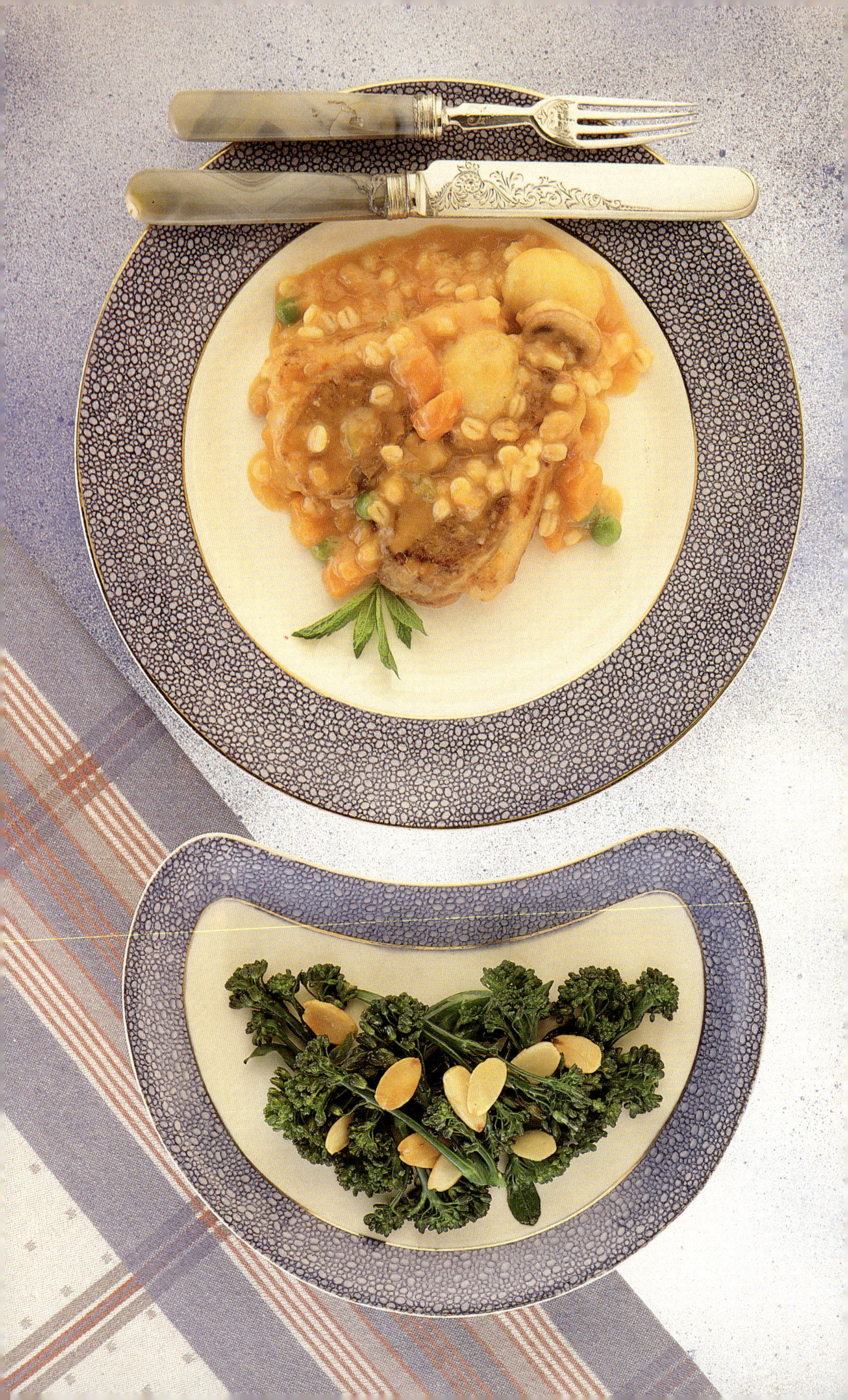

Navarin of Lamb

A casserole ensuring tender lamb with plenty of good vegetable flavours.

15 minutes
Preparation time

Cooking time:
1 hour

Serves 4

a little oil
1 onion, peeled and chopped
900 g (2 lb) best end of lamb
295 g (10.4 oz) Campbell's Condensed Vegetable Soup
1 tbsp tomato puree
salt and freshly ground black pepper
1 bouquet garni
10 button mushrooms, wiped
10 small new potatoes, washed
Garnish: sprig of mint

Preheat the oven, 160°C (325°F) or Gas 3. Heat the oil in a casserole and add the onion. Fry for 3 minutes. Add the lamb and brown on each side. Add remaining ingredients and stir well. Cover and cook in the oven for 1 hour or until the meat is tender.

Serve with green beans, broccoli or mange tout.

(F) 3 months

[M] 8 minutes on high and 5 minutes standing time

Cook's notes:

15 *minutes*
Preparation time

Cooking time:
2 hours

Serves 4-6

Beefy Meat Loaf

This is very good for a picnic or a salad type lunch in the garden. Alternatively, it can be served hot in the winter with a can of Campbell's Condensed Cream of Tomato Soup poured over as a sauce. A good recipe to prepare in advance.

185 g (6 oz) breadcrumbs
450 g (1 lb) minced beef or lamb
295 g (10.4 oz) Campbell's Condensed French Onion Soup
1 teasp mixed herbs
1 tbsp Worcestershire sauce
2 eggs
freshly ground black pepper

Preheat the oven, 160°C (325°F) or Gas 3. Mix all ingredients together and put into a greased 900 ml (1½ pint) loaf tin and cover with foil. Bake in the oven for 2 hours. Leave in the tin for 10 minutes and then turn out. Eat either hot or cold.

Serve with potatoes and salad.

(F)   3 months

[M]   8-10 minutes on high in microwave container

Cook's notes:

Sausage and Kidney Sauté

A lovely supper dish, very quick to make and good with a steaming hot baked potato. Try to buy freshly made herb sausages as they will add flavour to the dish, otherwise add a pinch of your favourite herb.

15 *minutes*
Preparation time

Cooking time:
15 minutes

Serves 4

a little oil
4 rashers streaky bacon, derinded and chopped
1 large onion, peeled and chopped
225 g (8 oz) herb sausages
225 g (8 oz) calf's kidney, halved and core removed
295 g (10.4 oz) Campbell's Condensed Oxtail Soup
150 ml (¼ pint) water
2 tbsp red wine
Garnish: chopped parsley

Heat the oil in a saucepan and add the bacon and onion. Fry over a low heat for 3 minutes. Add the sausages and brown on all sides. Add the kidneys and then add the soup, water and wine. Cover and cook for 15 minutes. Arrange in a warmed serving dish and garnish with parsley.

Serve with triangles of toast and a green salad, or baked potatoes.

Cook's notes:

FOR DAILY HITS · 55

15 *minutes*
Preparation time

Cooking time:
30 minutes

Serves 6

Fish Pasties

Not quite a Cornish pasty but very like it, using fish instead of meat. Very easy to do and a lovely surprise at the table.

450 g (1 lb) packet puff pastry
450 g (1 lb) thickly cut cod fillet, skinned and cut into 6 pieces
125 g (4 oz) frozen prawns, thawed
295 g (10.4 oz) Campbell's Condensed Cream of Celery Soup
freshly ground black pepper
1 tbsp parsley, chopped
1 egg, beaten

Preheat the oven, 180°C (350°F) or Gas 4. Roll out the pastry thinly and cut into 6 rectangles about 12 cm (6 inches) × 8 cm (4 inches). Place one piece of fish on each and top with prawns, soup, pepper and parsley, dividing equally. Wet the edges of the pastry with water and fold up and seal. Place on a baking tray and brush with beaten egg. Cook in the oven for 30 minutes or until the pastry is golden brown.

Serve with a tomato salad or green beans.

Ⓕ   2 months

Cook's notes:

Chicken and Bacon Flan

Perfect for a picnic, lunch in the garden or whisked out of the deep freeze for the unexpected visitor.

15 minutes Preparation time

Cooking time: 45 minutes

Serves 4-6

225 g (8 oz) shortcrust pastry
4 rashers bacon, crisply grilled and cut into pieces
2 eggs
295 g (10.4 oz) Campbell's Condensed Cream of Chicken Soup
1 tbsp parsley
50 g (2 oz) Cheddar cheese, grated
¼ teasp thyme
freshly ground black pepper

Preheat the oven, 200°C (400°F) or Gas 6. Roll out the pastry to fit 23 cm (9 inch) quiche dish. Cover with foil, fill with baking beans and cook for 20 minutes. Meanwhile, mix all ingredients together. Remove the baking beans and foil and pour in the mixture. Cook for a further 25 minutes or until the mixture is set.

Serve with a raw spinach and avocado salad.

(F)   3 months

Cook's notes:

15 *minutes*
Preparation time

Cooking time:
45 minutes

Serves 4-6

Salmon and Asparagus Quiche

This highlights the delicate flavour of asparagus with fresh, canned or frozen salmon.

225 g (8 oz) shortcrust pastry
225 g (8 oz) canned, frozen or fresh salmon, cooked, boned and skinned
295 g (10.4 oz) Campbell's Condensed Asparagus Soup
juice of ½ lemon
freshly ground black pepper
a dash of Tabasco
2 eggs
50 g (2 oz) Cheddar cheese, grated
1 dessertsp parsley, chopped

Preheat the oven, 200°C (400°F) or Gas 6. Roll out the pastry to fit 23 cm (9 inch) quiche dish. Cover with foil, fill with baking beans and cook for 20 minutes. Meanwhile mix remaining ingredients together. Remove the baking beans and foil and pour into the pastry shell. Cook for a further 25 minutes or until the mixture is firm.

Ⓕ   2 months

Cook's notes:

Porky Pie

One of my favourite pies and unbelievably easy to cook. You can add kidney beans, sweetcorn, bacon or anything that you have left over in the kitchen. Experiment!

15 minutes Preparation time

Cooking time: 45 minutes

Serves 4-6

a little oil
2 onions, peeled and finely chopped
1 green pepper, cored and chopped
450 g (1 lb) sausage meat
300 g (10.6 oz) Campbell's Condensed Cream of Tomato Soup
1 dessertsp chopped parsley
450 g (1 lb) mashed potato, *or* 131 g (4$\frac{1}{2}$ oz) packet instant mash

Heat oil in a casserole, add the onion and pepper and fry for 3 minutes. Add the meat, soup and parsley and, stirring occasionally, cook for 30 minutes. Skim the fat off the top and put mixture into pie dish. Top with the potato and then put in a medium oven (180°C [350°F] or Gas 4) to heat through and brown the potato.

Serve with a green salad and granary bread.

(F)   3 months

Cook's notes:

10 minutes
Preparation time

Cooking time:
15 minutes

Serves 3-4

Turkey Risotto

A very hungry friend rang and said he was calling round for supper so I rushed to the larder and this was prepared in five minutes – what a quick and delicious way to impress!

6 rashers streaky bacon, chopped
1 onion, peeled and chopped roughly
350 g (12 oz) long grain rice
295 g (10.4 oz) Campbell's Condensed Turkey and Vegetable Soup
1 Campbell's Soup can of water
4 tbsp milk
freshly ground black pepper
1 tbsp chopped parsley

Fry bacon gently in a large frying pan to release the fat and then add the onion and cook for 3 minutes. Add the rice, stir and then add remaining ingredients. Cover and cook on a very low heat, stirring occasionally, for 15 minutes or until the rice is cooked.

Serve with a crisp green salad.

Ⓕ 3 months

Cook's notes:

Braised Brisket of Beef

This is particularly good for Sunday lunch. Prepare the vegetables the day before and then there is hardly anything to do on the day except put the casserole in the oven.

15 minutes
Preparation time

Cooking time:
2-2½ hours

Serves 6

1 tbsp oil
900 g (2 lb) brisket beef, rolled and tied
1 onion, peeled and finely chopped
1 leek, washed and chopped
1 clove garlic, peeled and crushed
1 teasp thyme
295 g (10.4 oz) Campbell's Condensed Vegetable Soup
150 ml (¼ pint) red wine

Preheat the oven, 160°C (325°F) or Gas 3. Heat the oil in a large casserole, add the beef and brown all over. Add the onion, leek, garlic and herbs and fry for a further 2 minutes. Add the soup and wine and mix well. Cover and cook in the oven for 2-2½ hours. Lift out the meat, slice and arrange on a warmed serving plate. Pour over the liquid and serve.

Serve with boiled potatoes and petit pois or Brussels sprouts. Also good with Layered Potatoes with Consomme *(see p.75).*

[M] 15 minutes on high plus 15 minutes standing time

Cook's notes:

10 minutes
Preparation time

Cooking time:
10-12 minutes

Serves 4

Spaghetti with Tuna

A very simple and delicious supper dish – good for eating in front of the telly!

450 g (1 lb) spaghetti
salt and freshly ground black pepper
185 g (6 oz) can tuna
295 g (10.4 oz) Campbell's Condensed Cream of Celery Soup
1 tbsp chopped parsley
grated Parmesan cheese

Cook the spaghetti in plenty of boiling salted water for 10-12 minutes and then drain. Mix remaining ingredients in a bowl and add to the spaghetti in the saucepan. Mix well, sprinkle with Parmesan to taste and serve.

Serve with a tomato salad sprinkled with chives or basil.

Cook's notes:

Beef Goulash

This dish is usually made from beef but you can use chicken, pork or veal instead. Add a few caraway seeds for extra flavour.

15 minutes
Preparation time

Cooking time:
1½ hours

Serves 4-6

700 g (1½ lb) stewing steak
1 tbsp oil
2 onions, peeled and finely chopped
3 teasp paprika
300 g (10.6 oz) Campbell's Condensed Cream of Tomato Soup
150 ml (¼ pint) water *or* half a can of Campbell's Condensed Consomme
1 tbsp lemon juice
125 g (4 oz) button mushrooms, wiped and sliced
freshly ground black pepper
150 ml (¼ pint) soured cream
Garnish: paprika

Preheat the oven, 150°C (300°F) or Gas 2. Cut beef into small cubes. Heat oil in a large casserole, add onions and paprika and cook for 3 minutes. Add beef and brown on all sides. Add the soup, water, lemon juice, mushrooms and pepper and stir well. Bring to the boil, cover and cook in the oven for 1½ hours or until the meat is tender. Swirl in the soured cream and sprinkle over some paprika.

Serve with noodles and a crisp green salad.

Ⓕ   2 months (**without soured cream**)

Cook's notes:

25 minutes
Preparation time

Cooking time:
10-15 minutes

Munchy Meatballs

I have chosen to make small meatballs which are good for children or as cocktail eats but if you want to make them a little larger, lower the oven temperature slightly and cook them longer. If you want a tomato sauce to serve with them, just use half a can of Campbell's Condensed Cream of Tomato Soup and add a little Worcestershire sauce.

450 g (1 lb) lean mince
1 teasp oregano
1 small egg
125 g (4 oz) fresh breadcrumbs
1 clove garlic, peeled and crushed
1 teasp lemon juice
half a can of 300 g (10.6 oz) Campbell's Condensed Tomato and Rice Soup

Preheat the oven, 200°C (400°F) or Gas 6. Mix all the ingredients together in a bowl. Using the palms of your hands roll out mince balls to the size of a small walnut. Place on an oiled baking tray and cook for about 10-15 minutes or until crisping slightly and brown.

Makes about 50 balls.

Serve on cocktail sticks or with a tomato sauce.

(F)   3 months

[M]   3 minutes on high

Cook's notes:

Oriental Calf's Liver

Try this quick and easy supper dish using Campbell's Condensed Vegetable Soup which saves preparing and pre-cooking vegetables.

1 tbsp oil
½ teasp curry powder
1 teasp oregano
450 g (1 lb) calf's liver, sliced
295 g (10.4 oz) Campbell's Condensed Vegetable Soup
150 ml (¼ pint) carton natural yoghurt
Garnish: chopped parsley

Heat the oil in a frying pan and add the curry powder and oregano. Cook gently for 2 minutes. Add the liver and the soup and cook for a further 5 minutes. Stir in the yoghurt and arrange on a warmed serving dish. Garnish with the parsley.

Serve with brown rice and freshly cooked spinach.

5 *minutes*
Preparation time

Cooking time:
10 minutes

Serves 3-4

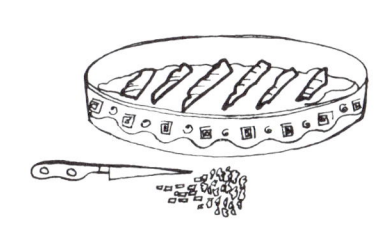

Cook's notes:

15 minutes
Preparation time

Cooking time:
35 minutes

Serves 4

Fish Pie

A delicious way to serve fish using Campbell's Condensed Cream of Celery as a lovely creamy sauce.

225 g (8 oz) smoked cod, deboned and skinned
225 g (8 oz) cod fillet, skinned
150 ml ($\frac{1}{4}$ pint) milk
125 g (4 oz) prawns, shelled
2 hard-boiled eggs, shelled and chopped
295 g (10.4 oz) Campbell's Condensed Cream of Celery Soup
50 g (2 oz) Cheddar cheese, grated
freshly ground black pepper
juice of 1 lemon
a dash of Tabasco
225 g (8 oz) packet puff pastry
milk for glaze

Preheat the oven, 200°C (400°F) or Gas 6. Poach the fish in the milk over a low heat for 10 minutes. Flake the fish and then stir in all ingredients except the pastry and put into a 1 litre (2 pint) pie dish. Roll out the pastry, wet the edges of the dish and cover with the pastry. Trim the edges and press down well. Brush with milk and bake in the oven for 25 minutes or until golden brown.

Serve with new potatoes and glazed carrots.

(F) 2 months

Cook's notes:

Pork and Haricot Casserole

A great hotpot and very quick to make. Using canned beans make it much easier as there is no need to soak the beans overnight.

15 minutes Preparation time

Cooking time: 45 minutes

Serves 4-6

a little oil
1 onion, peeled and finely chopped
1 clove garlic, peeled and crushed
450 g (1 lb) belly of pork, cut into cubes
6 cloves
225 g (8 oz) can haricot beans, drained
$\frac{1}{2}$ teasp dried mixed herbs
1 stick celery, chopped
300 g (10.6 oz) Campbell's Condensed Cream of Tomato Soup
225 g (8 oz) frankfurters, sliced
Garnish: chopped parsley

Heat oil in a casserole, add the onion and garlic and fry for 3 minutes. Add all the rest of the ingredients and mix well. Cover and cook on a low heat for 45 minutes or until the pork is tender. Garnish with the chopped parsley.

Serve with baked potatoes and petit pois.

(F) 3 months

[M] 10 minutes on high and 5 minutes standing time

Cook's notes:

15 *minutes*
Preparation time

Cooking time:
30 minutes

Serves 4

Cottage Pie

You can use up the weekend joint of lamb and call this dish shepherd's pie: the taste will be just as good. If you have any leftover cooked potatoes then use these up too but use instant mash if you are in a hurry.

295 g (10.4 oz) Campbell's Condensed Vegetable Soup
a little oil
1 onion, peeled and finely chopped
1 clove garlic, peeled and crushed
450 g (1 lb) lean mince
1 teasp Worcestershire sauce
1 teasp thyme
freshly ground black pepper
fresh or 131 g (4½ oz) packet instant mashed potato
Garnish: little freshly grated nutmeg

Preheat oven, 180°C (350°F) or Gas 4. Heat the oil in a pan and add the onion and garlic. Cook for 3 minutes over a low heat. Add the mince, soup, Worcestershire sauce, thyme, and pepper and stir well. Cook over a low heat for 5 minutes and test for seasoning. Place in a pie dish and top with the potato, roughing up the top with a fork. Sprinkle with the nutmeg and cook in the oven for 30 minutes.

Serve with broccoli.

(F)   2 months

For Globetrotters
Photograph pages 70-71

| Salami Cannelloni | Paella |
| Lamb Kebabs with Orange and Spice Rice | Prawn and Egg Curry |

Cook's notes:

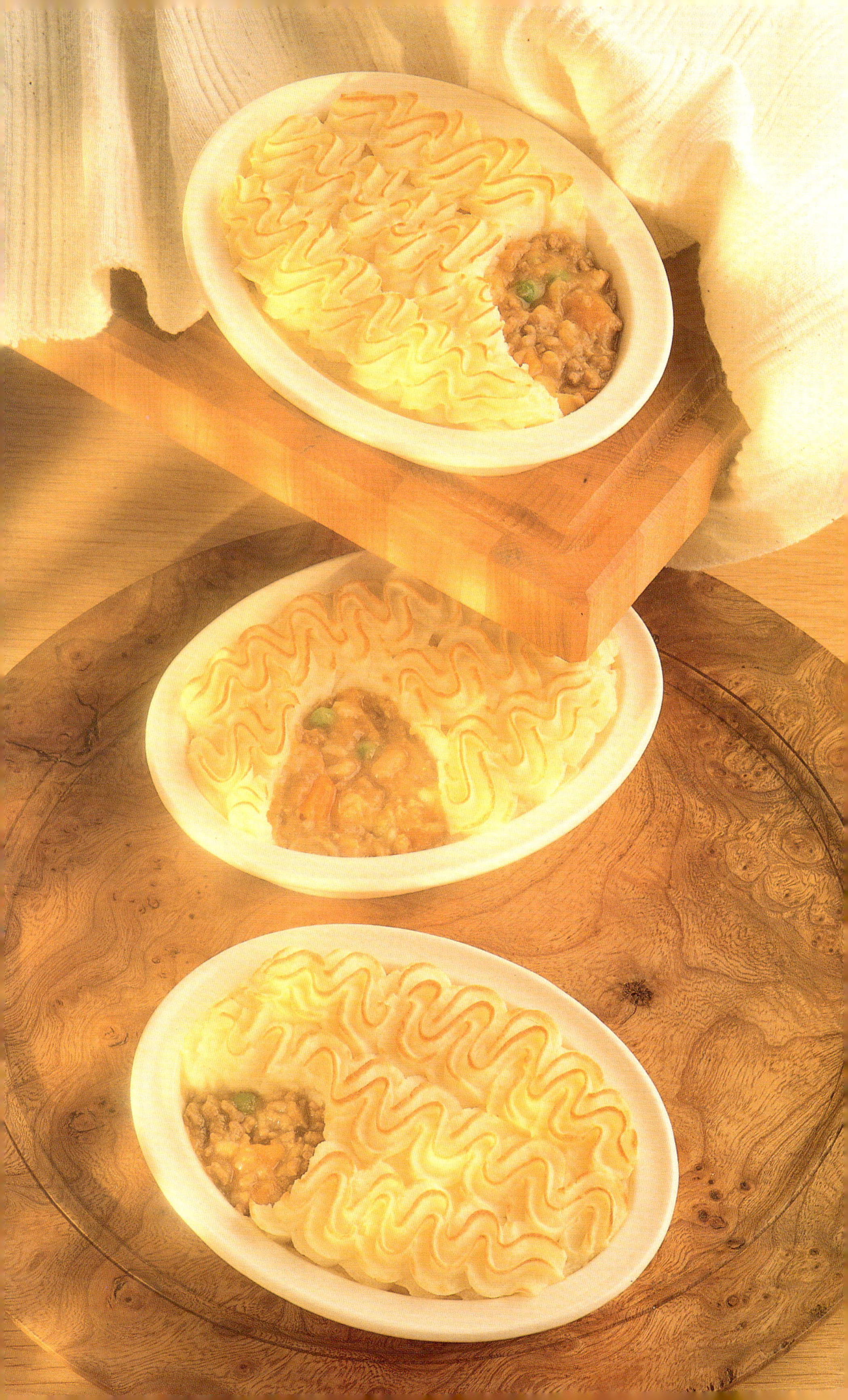

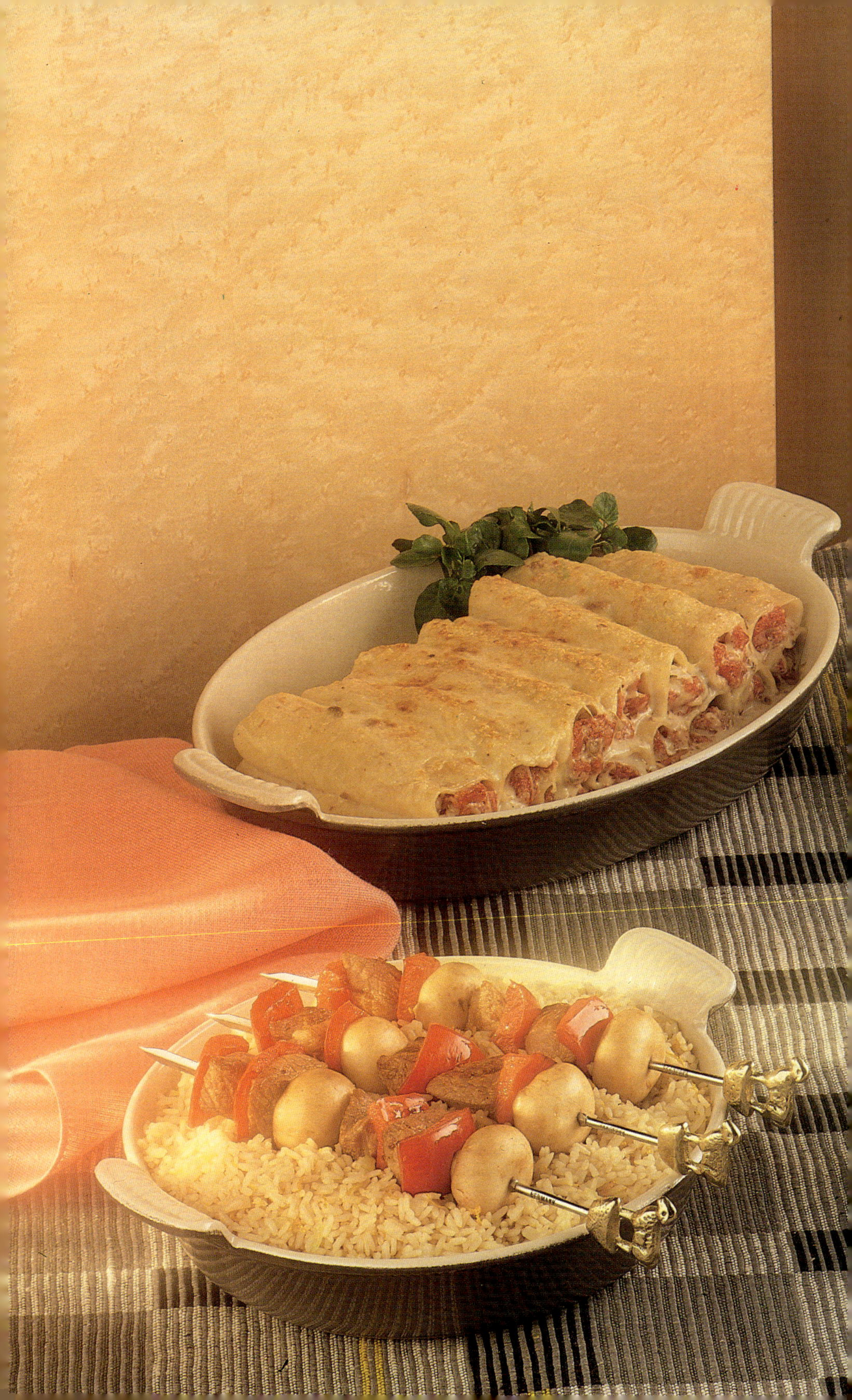

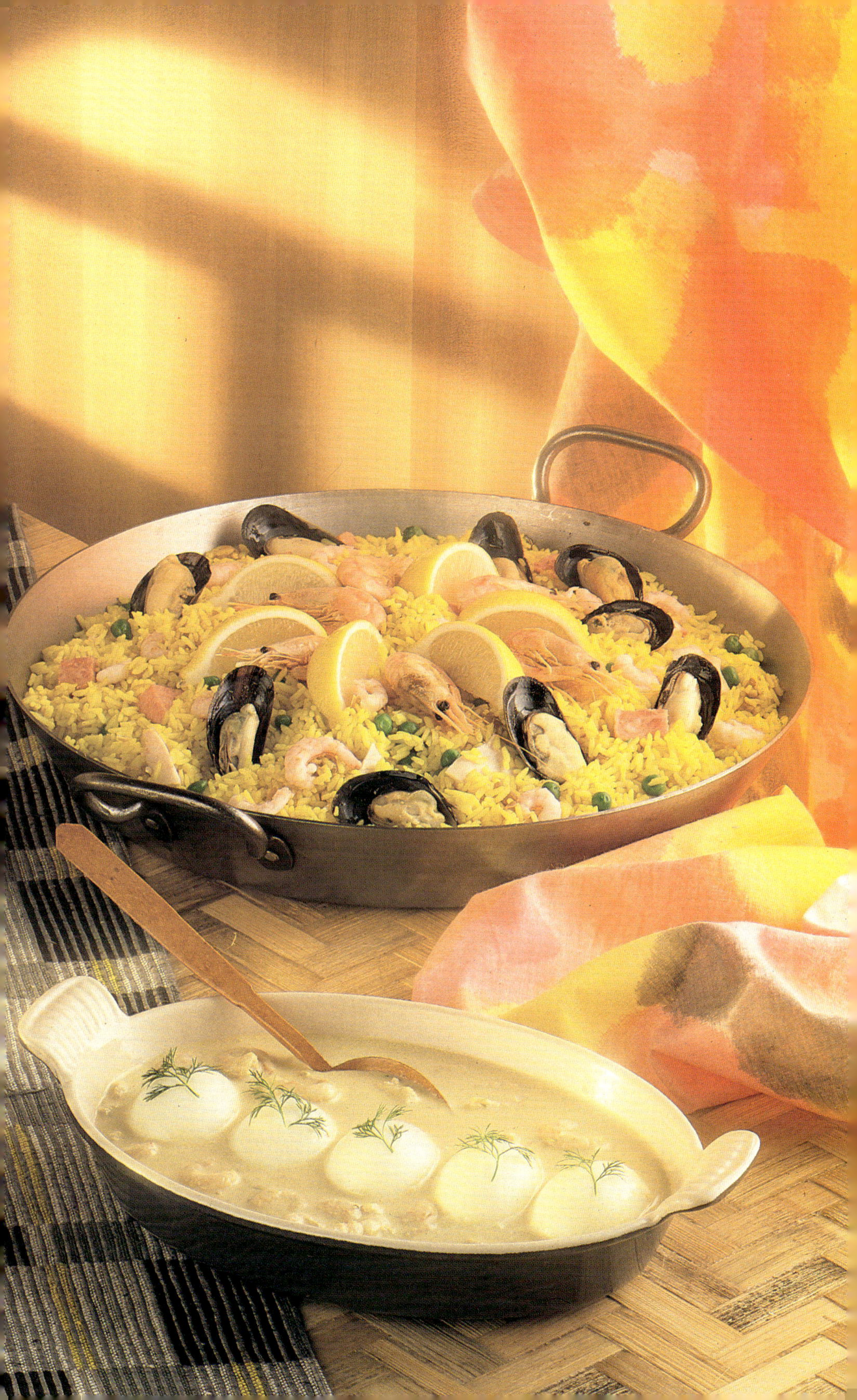

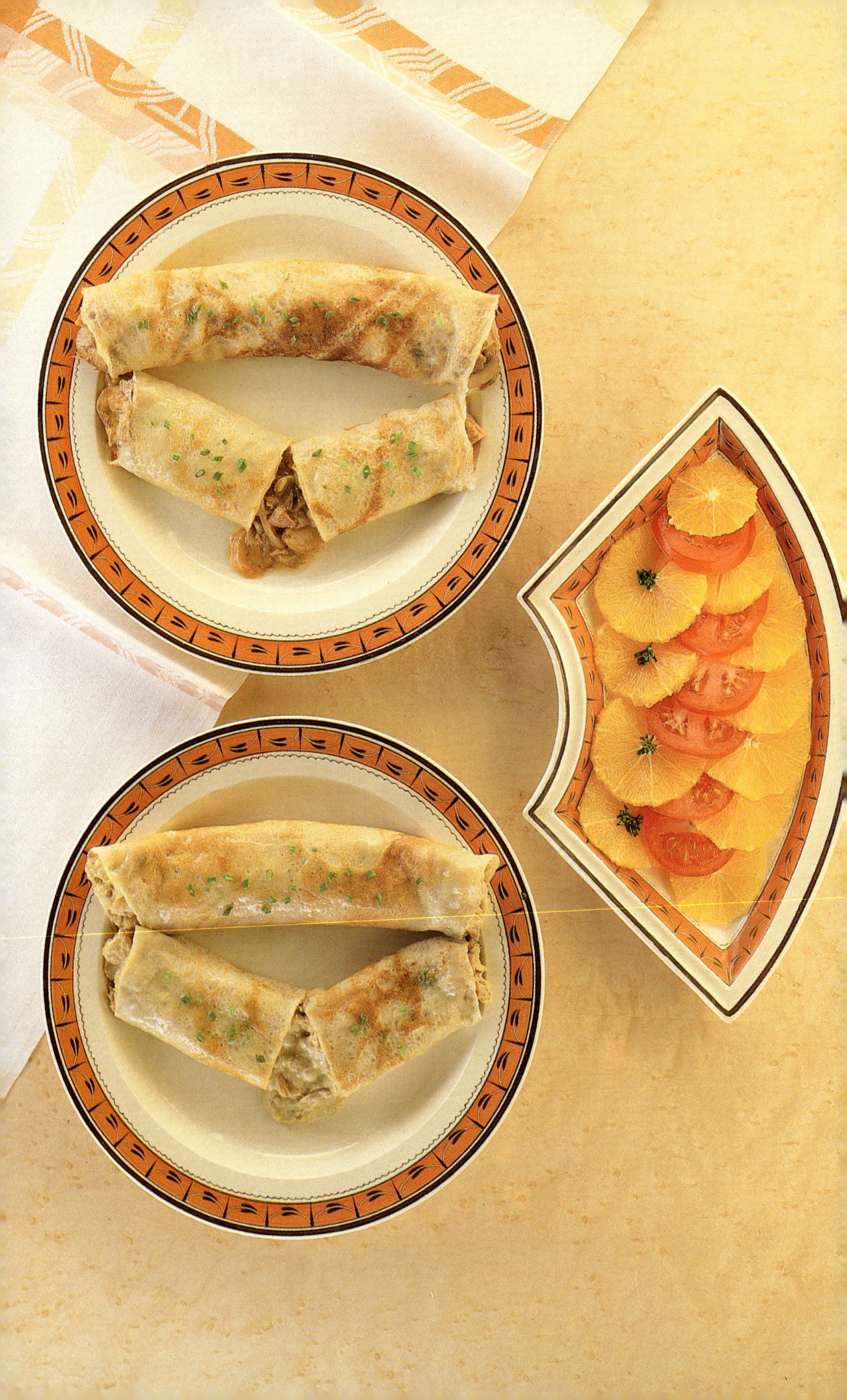

Stuffed Pancakes

You can make up the pancake mixture in advance and keep it in the fridge or freezer. It only takes a few minutes to make the filling.

To make pancakes
½ pint (300 ml) milk
125 g (4 oz) flour
pinch salt
1 egg
a few drops of oil
2 sprigs parsley, optional

Blend all ingredients together on high speed for 30 seconds. Leave to stand for half an hour. Heat a non-stick frying pan and using some absorbent kitchen paper soaked in oil, rub over the surface. When very hot, pour a serving spoonful of batter into the frying pan tilting it until the batter coats the pan evenly. Keep on a high heat for 20 seconds or until the edges start to curl and then toss or turn the pancake. Leave 10 seconds and then put onto an upturned plate and repeat until all the batter is used up. Cover with a damp cloth and keep warm on *very low* heat to prevent pancakes sticking.

15 minutes
Preparation time

Cooking time:
15 minutes
for pancakes

5 minutes
for stuffing

Serves 4

continued overleaf

Crab stuffing

295 g (10.4 oz) Campbell's Condensed Crab Bisque
198 g (7 oz) can tuna, drained
125 g (4 oz) button mushrooms, sliced
125 g (4 oz) beansprouts
Garnish: chives, finely chopped

Heat the soup and then add the tuna and mushrooms and cook over a low heat for 3 minutes. Add the bean sprouts and heat through. Put mixture onto each pancake and roll up. Fills 8 pancakes.

Salmon and asparagus stuffing

225 g (8 oz) can pink salmon
295 g (10.4 oz) Campbell's Condensed Asparagus Soup
3 tbsp double cream
a few drops of Tabasco
Garnish: chives, finely chopped

Mix all the ingredients together and heat over a low heat. Put the mixture onto each pancake and roll up. Fills 8 pancakes.

Serve with a tomato and orange salad.

Cook's notes:

Layered Potatoes with Consomme

This adds a good beefy flavour to the potatoes and makes a lovely change from a milky base.

25 g (1 oz) butter
450 g (1 lb) potatoes, peeled and thinly sliced
295 g (10.4 oz) Campbell's Condensed Consomme
freshly ground black pepper
a little freshly grated nutmeg
50 g (2 oz) Cheddar cheese, grated

Preheat the oven, 180°C (350°F) or Gas 4. Grease an ovenproof dish with the butter and then put in a layer of potatoes. Pour in half the consomme, sprinkle over a little pepper, nutmeg and half the cheese. Layer the rest of the potatoes on top and then season again. Pour in the rest of the consomme and top with the cheese. Bake in the oven for 1 hour or until the potatoes are cooked.

Serve with Braised Brisket of Beef *(see page 61)* or a similar meat dish.

15 minutes
Preparation time

Cooking time:
1 hour

Serves 4-6

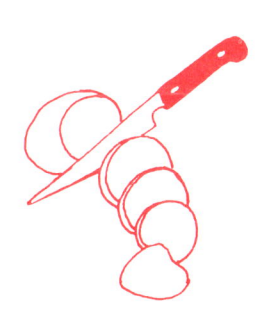

Cook's notes:

15 minutes
Preparation time

Cooking time:
10-15 minutes

Serves 6

Scotch Salmon with Prawn Sauce

This makes a delightful lunch or supper, particularly if you feel like something a little bit special.
Frozen salmon or cod steaks are very good value but make sure they are well thawed before cooking.

6 Scotch salmon or cod steaks about 125 g (4 oz) each
25 g (1 oz) butter
295 g (10.4 oz) Campbell's Condensed Cream of Smoked Salmon Soup
juice of ½ lemon
1 tbsp white wine, optional
4 oz peeled prawns, thawed
freshly ground black pepper
Garnish: sprigs of dill, paprika

Preheat the oven, 180°C (350°F) or Gas 4. Place the steaks in a buttered ovenproof dish and cover. Bake in the oven for about 10 minutes or until just cooked. Place in a serving dish and keep warm. Put the soup in a saucepan. Add the remaining ingredients. Stir, warming through, and pour over the salmon steaks. Garnish with spring onions, prawns and a sprinkle of paprika.

Serve with buttered new potatoes, French beans and courgettes.

[M] 8 minutes on high

Cook's notes:

FOR GLOBETROTTERS

Don't wait
for your next holiday
abroad to enjoy some of
your favourite foreign food. Campbell's
make it easy to produce dishes
with an authentic foreign
flavour all the year
round.

15 minutes
Preparation time

Cooking time:
25 minutes

Serves 4

Seafood Lasagne

You may use any of your favourite seafoods instead of my suggestions. For example, squid, mussels or even lobster if you are feeling rich! Try to buy the lasagne that needs no previous cooking but if you can't then use the uncooked kind and just boil in salted water for 5 minutes. Add a drop of oil to stop the sheets from sticking.

295 g (10.4 oz) Campbell's Condensed Crab Bisque
125 g (4 oz) cockles, shelled
125 g (4 oz) prawns, shelled
198 g (7 oz) can tuna
3 tomatoes, skinned and chopped
a dash of Tabasco
1 teasp Worcestershire sauce
freshly ground black pepper
a little lemon juice to taste
185 g (6 oz) lasagne
156 g (5½ oz) Campbell's Condensed Cream of Mushroom Soup
150 ml (¼ pint) natural yoghurt
50 g (2 oz) Cheddar cheese, grated
½ teasp mustard

Preheat the oven, 200°C (400°F) or Gas 6. Put the soup into a bowl, add the seafood, tomatoes, Tabasco, Worcestershire sauce, pepper and lemon juice and mix well. Grease a shallow ovenproof dish and pour in half the mixture. Lay over a layer of lasagne and top with rest of seafood mixture. Lay over rest of lasagne. Mix remaining ingredients together and spread on the top, covering well. Cook in the oven for about 25 minutes or until golden brown and bubbling.

Serve with a crisp green salad.

(F)   2 months

Cook's notes:

Salami Cannelloni

An all-Italian dish, easy to make and a great favourite. A distinguishing feature is the addition of salami.

125 g (4 oz) cannelloni
a little oil
1 onion, peeled and chopped
freshly ground black pepper
185 g (6 oz) salami, finely chopped
295 g (10.4 oz) Campbell's Condensed Cream of Mushroom Soup
juice of ½ lemon
a little Worcestershire sauce
50 g (2 oz) Bel Paese, or Cheddar cheese, thinly sliced
3 tbsp milk or cream
Garnish: grated Parmesan cheese and chopped parsley or a bunch of watercress

Preheat the oven, 180°C (350°F) or Gas 4. Cook cannelloni in boiling salted water for 5 minutes and then drain. Meanwhile, fry the onion in the oil for 3 minutes and then add the rest of the ingredients using only half the soup. Mix well. Use a teaspoon to stuff the cannelloni and place in an overproof dish. Mix the rest of the soup with the lemon juice, Worcestershire sauce, cheese and milk and then pour over the top. Bake in the oven for 35 minutes or until golden brown. Garnish with the Parmesan and chopped parsley and serve.

Serve with a crisp salad and chunks of granary bread.

(F)   3 months

15 minutes
Preparation time

**Cooking time:
40 minutes**

Serves 4

**Photograph:
page 70**

Cook's notes:

FOR GLOBETROTTERS

15 minutes Preparation time

Cooking time: 1½ hours

Serves 4

Osso Bucco

Italy is the homeland of this inexpensive stew of veal shin. The delicate flavour of bone marrow makes it extra delicious.

1 tbsp oil
1 onion, peeled and finely chopped
1 clove garlic, peeled and crushed
900 g (2 lb) shin veal, cut into pieces
295 g (10.4 oz) Campbell's Condensed Golden Vegetable Soup
½ teasp rosemary
150 ml (¼ pint) white wine or water
198 g (7 oz) can tomatoes
Garnish: 1 tbsp chopped parsley, grated rind of 1 lemon

Using a large frying pan with lid, heat the oil and add onion and garlic. Fry for 3 minutes and then add the meat and brown on both sides. Stir in the rest of the ingredients, cover and cook on a very low heat for 1½ hours. Mix the parsley and lemon rind together and sprinkle over the top.

Serve with rice or buttered noodles.

Ⓕ   2 months

Cook's notes:

Gnocchi

Gnocchi are small dumplings made from a flour, semolina or potato base. I have chosen the Roman way, using semolina, because it is the quickest method and the one with the most flavour. Anti semolina eaters don't be put off – it tastes nothing like the pudding you may remember from your school days.

15 minutes
Preparation time

Setting time:
1 hour

Cooking time:
30 minutes

Serves 8

295 g (10.4 oz) Campbell's Condensed Cream of Chicken Soup
150 ml (¼ pint) milk, or a little more if necessary
1 bayleaf
2½ tbsp semolina
25 g (1 oz) butter
25 g (1 oz) Cheddar cheese, grated
freshly ground black pepper
½ teasp dried mustard
1 teasp fresh parsley, chopped
Garnish: 25 g (1 oz) grated cheese and a little butter

Mix the soup, milk and bayleaf in a saucepan. Heat. Add the semolina, butter, cheese, pepper, mustard and parsley and simmer for 2 minutes stirring frequently. Remove the bayleaf. Put the mixture into an oiled Swiss roll tin, or equivalent, and spread the mixture evenly to make it about 1 cm (½ inch) thick. Leave for 1 hour until the paste is cold and set firmly. Cut the paste into walnut-size pieces and roll each into a ball. Heat the oven, 200°C (400°F) or Gas 6. Place in a buttered ovenproof dish, sprinkle over the cheese and add the butter in small knobs. Cook in the oven for about half an hour or until bubbling and golden in colour.

Serve with a crunchy lettuce and tomato salad.

(F)   2 months

Cook's notes:

20 minutes
Preparation time

**Cooking time:
20 minutes**

Serves 6

**Photograph:
page 71**

Paella

The Spanish usually take hours to prepare this sumptuous dish. This way is just as tasty and takes only minutes.

295 g (10.4 oz) Campbell's Condensed French Onion Soup
1 teasp saffron or turmeric
salt and freshly ground black pepper
2 cans water
350 g (12 oz) long grain rice
1 medium-sized cooked chicken, boned and chopped
1 tbsp parsley, chopped
225 g (8 oz) peas, cooked
600 ml (1 pint) mussels, cooked in their shells
185 g (6 oz) shelled prawns, cooked
125 g (4 oz) garlic sausage, chopped
Garnish: 6 whole prawns
1 lemon cut into 6 wedges

Put the soup, saffron or turmeric, salt and pepper, water and rice into a casserole or large frying pan. Cover, bring to the boil and simmer for 10 minutes. Add all remaining ingredients, stir well and leave over a low heat for 10 minutes to warm through. Garnish with the whole prawns and lemon wedges and serve.

Serve with a green salad with green olives and fennel.

Cook's notes:

Beef Bourguignon

Perfect for using up leftover red wine!

185 g (6 oz) streaky bacon, sliced
900 g (2 lb) stewing steak, cut into cubes
2 cloves garlic, peeled and crushed
295 g (10.4 oz) Campbell's Condensed French Onion Soup
2 tbsp brandy
bouquet garni
freshly ground black pepper
300 ml (½ pint) red wine
10 shallots, peeled and finely chopped
125 g (4 oz) button mushrooms, wiped and sliced
chopped parsley

Preheat the oven, 160°C (325°F) or Gas 3. Fry the bacon in a casserole, add the meat and brown on all sides. Add the shallots and garlic and fry for 1 minute. Add the remaining ingredients stirring well. Cover and cook in the oven for 1-1½ hours or until the meat is tender. Remove the bouquet garni and serve.

Serve with rice and glazed carrots.

(F)   3 months

15 minutes
Preparation time

Cooking time:
1-1½ hours

Serves 4

Cook's notes:

15 *minutes*
Preparation time

Cooking time:
1½ hours

Serves 8

Cassoulet

This French peasant dish is a most splendid casserole. The preparation is very simple and the flavour is well-balanced if cooked in the quantity suggested. Any leftovers will freeze well.

450 g (1 lb) haricot beans, canned
450 g (1 lb) belly of pork, cut into small chunks
450 g (1 lb) herb sausages, cut into small chunks
1 onion, peeled and chopped
2 cloves garlic, peeled and crushed
300 g (10.6 oz) Campbell's Condensed Cream of Tomato Soup
295 g (10.4 oz) Campbell's Condensed Vegetable Soup
6 small chicken joints
6 tbsp fresh white breadcrumbs

Preheat the oven, 160°C (325°F) or Gas 3. Put all the ingredients, except the breadcrumbs, into a large heavy earthenware casserole dish. Stir gently and then cover with water. Put on a lid and cook for 1 hour. Check water level once during cooking time. Remove the lid, sprinkle over the breadcrumbs and put back in the oven, uncovered, for a final 30 minutes and then serve straight from the pot.

Serve with chunks of warmed French bread and a green salad.

(F)   3 months

Cook's notes:

84 · FOR GLOBETROTTERS

Moussaka

The good old Greek favourite that most people love. It is the perfect dish for entertaining because once it is cooked it can only improve if left in a low oven.

1 teasp salt
450 g (1 lb) aubergines, thinly sliced
oil for frying
1 large onion, peeled and chopped
1 clove garlic, peeled and crushed
450 g (1 lb) lean mince
300 g (10.6 oz) Campbell's Condensed Cream of Tomato Soup
150 ml ($1/4$ pint) water or red wine
1 teasp oregano
freshly ground black pepper
156 g ($5\frac{1}{2}$ oz) Campbell's Condensed Mushroom Soup
2 eggs
3 tbsp milk or cream
50 g (2 oz) Cheddar cheese, grated.

Preheat the oven, 180°C (350°F) or Gas 4. Sprinkle the salt over the aubergine slices. Leave for 5 minutes, rinse and then dry. Fry the aubergine in the oil and remove. Add the onion and garlic and fry for 2 minutes. Add the mince, tomato soup, water or wine, oregano and pepper and stir well. Place a layer of aubergine in a greased ovenproof dish and then spoon over half the meat mixture. Add another layer of aubergine and then the rest of the meat. Top with a layer of aubergine. Mix the mushroom soup, eggs, milk or cream and cheese together and pour over the top. Cook for about 35 minutes or until bubbling and golden brown.

Serve with a mixed green salad including black olives and fetta cheese.

(F)   2 months

25 minutes
Preparation time

Cooking time:
35 minutes

Serves 6

Cook's notes:

15 *minutes*
Preparation time

**Cooking time:
20 minutes**

**Photograph:
page 70**

Lamb Kebabs with Orange and Spiced Rice

Skewered chunks of meat normally cooked over a charcoal grill but equally good cooked under an ordinary grill.

Rice
a little oil
1 onion, peeled and finely chopped
225 g (8 oz) long grain rice
295 g (10.4 oz) Campbell's Condensed Consomme
juice of 2 oranges
a little fresh grated ginger
$\frac{1}{4}$ teasp ground coriander
$\frac{1}{4}$ teasp ground cumin

Kebabs
450 g (1 lb) boned shoulder of lamb, cubed
125 g (4 oz) button mushrooms, wiped
1 red pepper, cored, deseeded and chopped into chunks

Sauce
150 ml ($\frac{1}{2}$ pint) natural yoghurt
1 dessertsp fresh mint, chopped finely

Heat the oil, add onion and fry for 3 minutes. Add all the rest of the rice ingredients, cover and simmer for 10 minutes or until cooked. Meanwhile, thread meat, mushrooms and peppers onto skewers and cook under a hot grill turning frequently. Mix the yoghurt and mint together. Place the rice on a warmed serving dish. Arrange the kebabs on the rice and pour over the yoghurt sauce.

Serve with a tomato and fetta cheese salad.

Cook's notes:

Sweet & Sour Prawns

A very quick and easy way to give prawns a Chinese flavour. Saffron or turmeric added to the rice will give a subtle touch of colour to the dish.

15 minutes
Preparation time

**Cooking time:
5 minutes**

Serves 4-6

a little oil
1 onion, peeled and finely chopped
1 carrot, peeled and finely chopped
1 small green pepper, cored and chopped
300 g (10.6 oz) Campbell's Cream of Tomato Soup
1 tbsp vinegar
1 tbsp Soya sauce
1 small can pineapple chunks, drained
450 g (1 lb) prawns, peeled

Heat oil, add onion and cook for 3 minutes. Add all remaining ingredients and heat through.

Serve on a bed of saffron or tumeric rice.

Cook's notes:

15 minutes
Preparation time

**Cooking time:
20 minutes**

Serves 2-3

Canton Fish Dish

Cantonese cooking often features fish as it is readily available from local fishermen. This dish is very low in calories, easy to prepare and has a marvellous combination of flavours.

900 g (2 lb) whole turbot, haddock, bass or plaice, head and tail removed
1 piece root ginger, peeled and grated
2 spring onions, finely chopped
50 g (2 oz) beansprouts, canned or fresh
50 g (2 oz) button mushrooms, wiped and sliced
1 clove garlic, peeled and crushed
1 tbsp Soya sauce
295 g (10.4 oz) Campbell's Condensed Consomme
Garnish: lemon and parsley

Preheat the oven, 180°C (350°F) or Gas 4. Place the fish in an ovenproof dish. Add remaining ingredients, cover and bake in the oven for about 20 minutes or until the fish is firm but cooked.

Serve with very lightly cooked crispy mange tout.

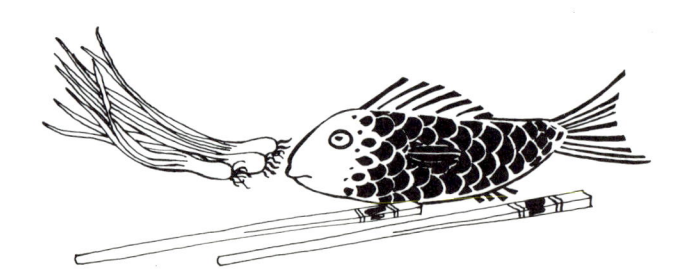

Cook's notes:

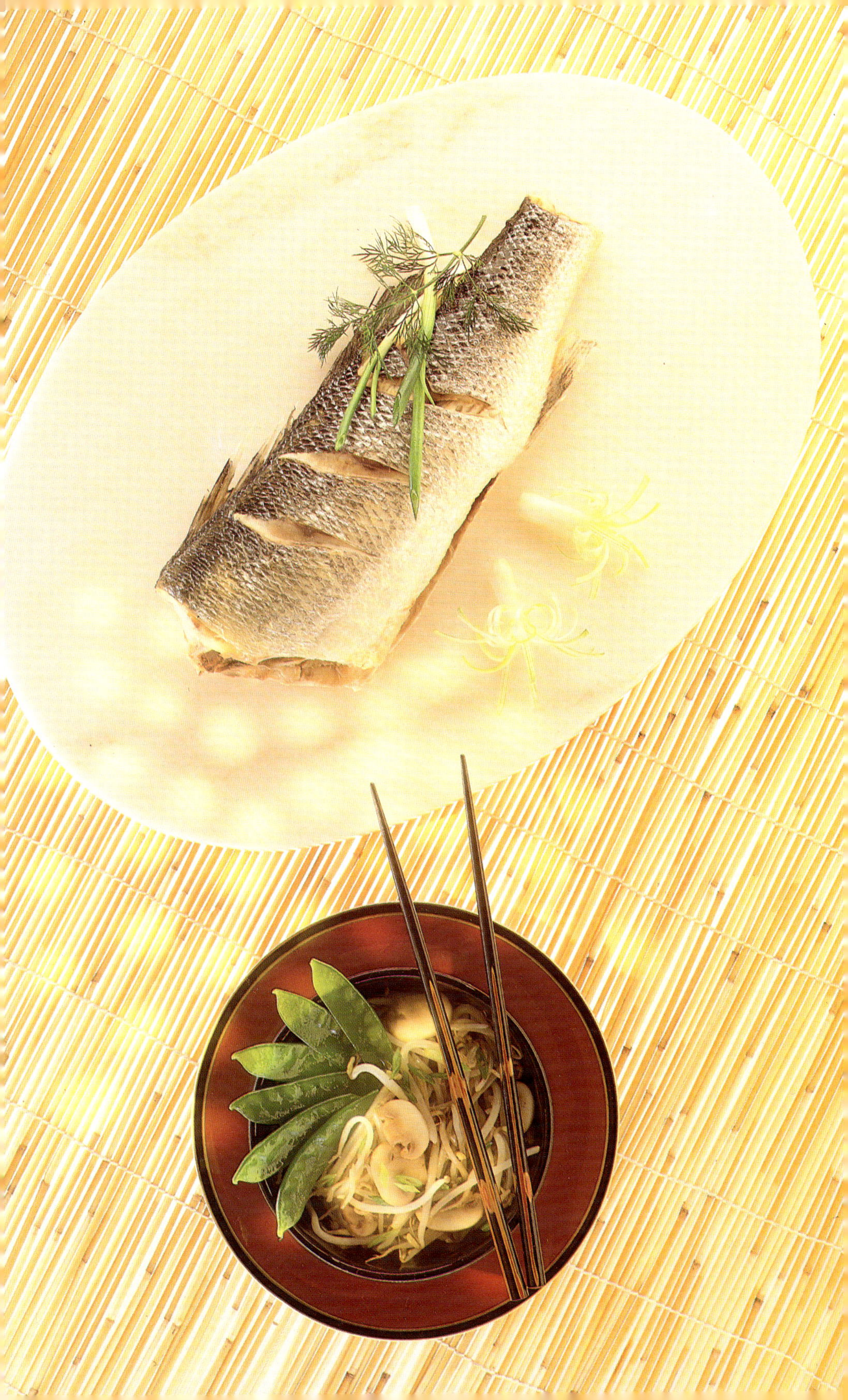

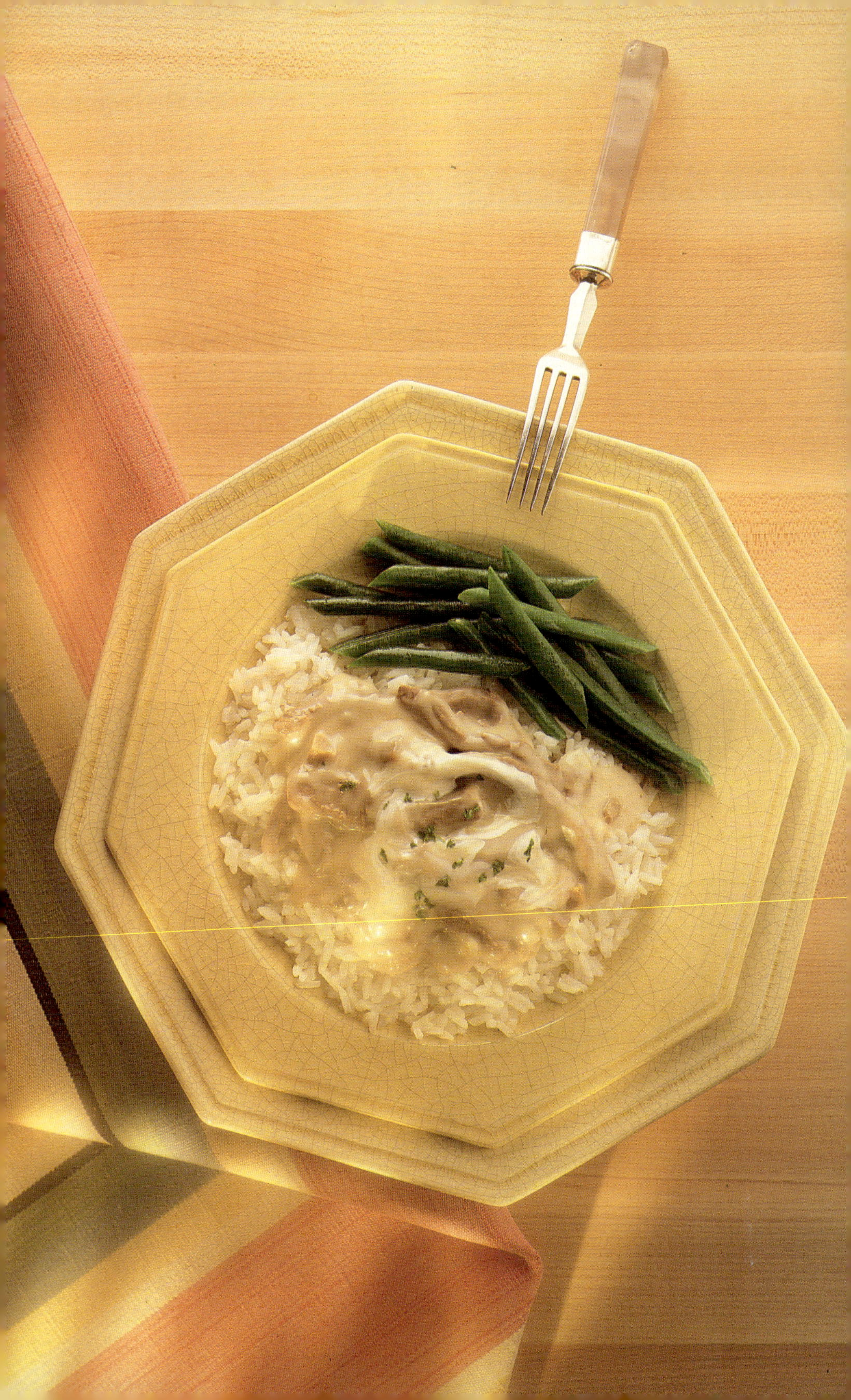

Beef Strogonoff

A good Hungarian favourite and very simple to make. It is worth using good steak as it is only cooked for a few minutes.

15 minutes
Preparation time

Cooking time:
10 minutes

Serves 4

1 onion, peeled and finely chopped
a little oil
450 g (1 lb) fillet or rump steak, cut into thin strips
1 teasp tomato puree
295 g (10.4 oz) Campbell's Condensed Cream of Mushroom Soup
freshly ground black pepper
150 ml (¼ pint) soured cream
Garnish: a little chopped parsley

Use a large frying pan. Fry the onion in the oil for 2 minutes. Add the meat and cook for 5 minutes. Add the remaining ingredients, except the soured cream, and stir well. Cook for 5 minutes and then swirl in the soured cream and serve garnished with the parsley.

Serve with boiled rice and green beans or hot beetroot.

Ⓕ 2 months (**without soured cream**)

Cook's notes:

15 *minutes*
Preparation time

Cooking time:
1 hour

Serves 4

Pork Paprika

This is another Hungarian dish, easy to prepare and with a very unusual and interesting flavour.

2 tbsp oil
1 onion, peeled and finely chopped
450 g (1 lb) lean pork cut into 2.5 cm (1 inch) cubes
295 g (10.4 oz) Campbell's Condensed Cream of Celery Soup
350 g (12 oz) jar Hungarian shredded peppers
freshly ground black pepper
½ teasp ground cumin
pinch ground cloves
50 g (2 oz) stuffed olives, sliced (optional)

Preheat the oven, 160°C (325°F) or Gas 3. Heat oil in casserole. Add onion and cook for 3 minutes. Add pork and stir over heat for 2 minutes. Add all remaining ingredients. Cover and cook in the oven for 1 hour, or until the meat is tender.

Serve on a bed of rice with green vegetables.

Ⓕ   2 months

Cook's notes:

West Indian Risotto

An exotic and original dish combining foods like bananas, hot chilli sauce and coconut (enhanced by the accompaniment of a long cool rum punch!).

15 minutes
Preparation time

Cooking time:
5 minutes

Serves 4

1 tbsp oil
1 onion, peeled and finely chopped
1 clove garlic, peeled and crushed
185 g (6 oz) long grain rice, cooked
156 g (5½ oz) Campbell's Condensed Cream of Celery Soup
1 small red pepper, cored and finely chopped
185 g (6 oz) peeled prawns
1 teasp chilli sauce, or more if you wish!
juice of 1 lime
freshly ground black pepper
2 bananas, peeled and sliced
Garnish: flaked coconut

Heat the oil. Add onion and garlic and fry for 3 minutes. Add the remaining ingredients and mix well. Cook over a low heat for 5 minutes and then serve. Garnish with coconut.

Served with boiled okra (lady's fingers).

Cook's notes:

FOR GLOBETROTTERS · 93

15 minutes
Preparation time

Cooking time:
30 minutes

Serves 6-8

Bobotie

This is a delicious African variation of Moussaka using curry to flavour the juices. It is perfect for entertaining or feeding a busy family as it can be left in the oven without spoiling.

1 tbsp oil
2 onions, peeled and sliced
900 g (2 lb) mince
295 g (10.4 oz) Campbell's Condensed Consomme
¼ teasp ground cloves
1 teasp turmeric
1 tbsp vinegar
½ teasp nutmeg
1 teasp ground ginger
2 teasp curry powder
1 dessertsp chutney or apricot jam
1 dessertsp sugar

Topping
2 eggs, beaten
150 ml (¼ pint) milk

Preheat the oven, 180°C (350°F) or Gas 4. Heat oil in a pan, add the onions and fry for 2 minutes. Add the mince and consomme and simmer for 5 minutes. Add all the remaining ingredients and stir well. Pour into an ovenproof dish and smooth over the top. Mix the eggs and milk together and pour over the meat mixture. Bake in the oven for 30 minutes and then turn to a low heat until ready to eat.

Serve with saffron or turmeric rice, with a few raisins added, and a green salad.

(F)   2 months

Cook's notes:

Chicken Casserole with Peanuts

A lovely Brazilian dish using peanut butter to flavour the chicken.

15 minutes
Preparation time

Cooking time: 1 hour

Serves 4

1½ kg (3 lb) chicken, jointed
1 tbsp peanut butter
a little oil
1 onion, peeled and finely chopped
2 cloves garlic, peeled and crushed
4 spring onions, chopped
295 g (10.4 oz) Campbell's Condensed Cream of Celery Soup
freshly ground black pepper
juice of ½ lemon
1 green pepper, cored and finely chopped
1 tbsp parsley, chopped
150 ml (¼ pint) coconut milk or water
a dash of Tabasco

Preheat the oven, 180°C (350°F) or Gas 4. Dry the chicken joints and spread with peanut butter. Heat the oil, add the onion, garlic and spring onions and fry for 3 minutes. Add the remaining ingredients and stir carefully. Cover and cook for 1 hour or until the chicken is cooked.

Serve with brown rice and a crunchy green vegetable.

(F)   3 months

[M]   8 minutes on high and 10 minutes standing time

Cook's notes:

FOR GLOBETROTTERS

15 minutes
Preparation time

**Cooking time:
30 minutes**

Serves 4

Chocolate Chilli Con Carne

This is a very surprising way of using chocolate! It adds a wonderful nutty flavour and gives a beautiful glaze to a savoury dish.

1 tbsp oil
1 onion, peeled and chopped
450 g (1 lb) mince
2 × 295 g (10.4 oz) cans red kidney beans, drained
300 g (10.6 oz) Campbell's Condensed Cream of Tomato Soup
1 level teasp chilli powder
25 g (1 oz) dark chocolate, grated

Heat the oil in a casserole, add the onion and fry for 3 minutes. Add the remaining ingredients and stir well. Simmer over a low heat for 30 minutes stirring occasionally.

Serve with warm crusty bread and a tossed green salad.

(F)· 3 months

M 8 minutes on high

Cook's notes:

Chicken Curry

This is one of the most satisfactory short-cuts to a good curry. If you have the time, serve it with all the goodies like peanuts, yoghurt and cucumber, poppadoms, coconut and bananas.

15 minutes Preparation time

Cooking time: 15 minutes

Serves 4

1 tbsp oil
1 large onion, peeled and finely chopped
1 teasp curry powder
1/4 teasp ground coriander
1/4 teasp ground ginger
295 g (10.4 oz) Campbell's Condensed Turkey and Vegetable Broth
25 g (1 oz) sultanas
1 tbsp mango chutney
1 medium-sized cooked chicken, boned and chopped
150 ml (1/4 pint) soured cream

Heat oil in a pan, fry the onion for 2 minutes and then add the curry, coriander and ginger and fry for 3 minutes. Add the soup, sultanas, chutney and chicken and stir well. Add a little water if sauce is too thick. Cover and cook over low heat for 15 minutes. Stir in soured cream and serve.

Serve with rice and a crisp salad.

(F) 2 months

[M] 8 minutes on high and 10 minutes standing time

Cook's notes:

Prawn and Egg Curry

10 minutes
Preparation time

Cooking time:
5 minutes

Serves 4

Photograph:
page 71

This light curry could not be quicker or easier. A few prawns, some hard-boiled eggs, a can of Campbell's Condensed Asparagus Soup and some spices.

a little oil
1 onion, peeled and finely chopped
1 clove garlic, peeled and crushed
½ teasp curry powder
225 g (8 oz) frozen prawns, thawed
295 g (10.4 oz) Campbell's Condensed Asparagus Soup
juice of ½ lemon
4 hard-boiled eggs, shelled and halved

Heat the oil. Add the onion, garlic and curry powder and fry for 5 minutes on a low heat. Add the prawns and soup and stir well. Finally, add the lemon juice and the eggs. Heat through and serve.

Serve with rice and a mixed salad.

Cook's notes:

FOR WELL BEING

Maintaining a balanced diet when you're leading a busy life isn't always easy. So if you've been cutting corners try one of the recipes in this section. They have all been specially selected for their low fat content and provide a host of new ideas using fish, vegetables, poultry and white meat.

15 *minutes*
Preparation time

**Cooking time:
50 minutes**

Serves 4

Stuffed Onions

Onions are full of vitamin C and there will be no tears over this recipe as cooking the onions removes the acids contained in raw onions.

4 large onions, peeled
295 g (10.4 oz) Campbell's Condensed Cream of Celery Soup
3 tbsp fine brown breadcrumbs
2 tomatoes, skinned and chopped
1 teasp oregano
1 teasp fresh parsley, finely chopped
salt and freshly ground black pepper
50 g (2 oz) Cheddar cheese, grated

Preheat the oven, 180°C (350°F) or Gas 4. Cook the onions in boiling salted water for 20 minutes, drain and cool. Remove the centres with a teaspoon leaving about 3 layers of onion. In a bowl, mix half the soup, breadcrumbs, tomatoes, herbs and pepper. Chop up the onion middles and add to mixture. Stir and use to stuff the whole onions. Place on a baking tray, top with the remaining soup and the cheese, cover and bake in the oven for 30 minutes.

Serve with a watercress and raw mushroom salad.

(F)   2 months

[M]   10 minutes on high

Cook's notes:

Chicken and Bacon Soufflé

10 minutes
Preparation time

Cooking time:
20-25 minutes

Serves 4

You need never be afraid of making a soufflé if you follow three simple rules:

* make sure the oven is at the correct temperature;
* use Campbell's Condensed Soup undiluted as the consistency is perfect;
* make sure your 'eaters' are at the table when the soufflé comes out of the oven.

295 g (10.4 oz) Campbell's Condensed Cream of Chicken Soup
1 tbsp grated Parmesan cheese
4 rashers back bacon, fried crisp and chopped
½ teasp dried mustard
freshly ground black pepper
4 eggs, separated

Preheat the oven, 200°C (400°F) or Gas 6. Mix together all the ingredients, except the egg whites. Whisk the egg whites until very stiff and, using a metal spoon, fold into the soup mixture. Pour into a 1 litre (2 pint) greased soufflé dish and cook for 20-25 minutes or until the top is well risen and golden brown. Serve immediately.

Serve with a tomato salad.

Cook's notes:

10 minutes
Preparation time

**Cooking time:
20-25 minutes**

Serves 4

Crab and Cheese Soufflé

Here is a lovely seafood soufflé based on a cheesy sauce spiked with spice. Don't forget the three rules given for the previous recipe.

295 g (10.4 oz) Campbell's Condensed Crab Bisque
50 g (2 oz) Cheddar cheese, grated
a few drops of Tabasco
1 teasp Worcestershire sauce
freshly ground black pepper
4 eggs, separated

Preheat the oven, 200°C (400°F) or Gas 6. Mix all the ingredients together except the egg whites. Whisk the whites until very stiff and, using a metal spoon, fold into the soup mixture. Pour into a 1 litre (2 pint) greased soufflé dish and cook for 20-25 minutes or until the top is well risen and golden brown. Serve immediately.

Serve with a crisp green salad.

Cook's notes:

Moules Provençales

This is a typically French dish and is one of the best ways of serving mussels: in a garlic and tomato sauce. Bon appétit!

900 g (2 lb) fresh mussels
1 onion, peeled and finely chopped
2 cloves garlic, peeled and crushed
300 g (10.6 oz) Campbell's Condensed Cream of Tomato Soup
2 tbsp parsley, chopped
salt and freshly ground black pepper
5 tbsp white wine
Garnish: chopped parsley

It's important to scrub the mussels well. Remove all the beard (the stringy part attached to the shell) and set aside. Put remaining ingredients into a large saucepan and bring to the boil. Simmer for 3 minutes and then add the mussels. Bring back to the boil and simmer for 10 minutes or until the mussels have opened well. Serve piping hot in soup bowls with a garnish of parsley. N.B. *Discard any mussels that do not open as they may be bad.*

Serve with hot herb bread.

15 minutes Preparation time

Cooking time: 10 minutes

Serves 4

Cook's notes:

15 minutes
Preparation time

Cooking time:
10 minutes

Serves 4

Mushrooms à la Greque

This dish is very low in calories, quick to make and has a lovely fresh herb flavour.

1 tbsp oil
1 onion, peeled and finely chopped
salt and freshly ground black pepper
1 bayleaf
sprig of fresh thyme
225 g (8 oz) button mushrooms, wiped
1 dessertsp tomato puree
295 g (10.4 oz) Campbell's Condensed Consomme
Garnish: chopped parsley

Heat the oil, add the onion and cook for 3 minutes. Add remaining ingredients and stir well. Cover and simmer for 10 minutes. Remove the herbs and chill in fridge. Serve with the chopped parsley.

Serve with granary bread.

Cook's notes:

Plaice with Asparagus

Fresh or frozen plaice can be used. Remember to allow time for frozen fish to thaw. (If you are in a hurry, soak the pack in cold water for about 10 minutes.)
If you can't get fresh asparagus then you can always use frozen or canned.

15 minutes
Preparation time

Cooking time:
30 minutes

Serves 2-4

a little butter
4 fillets plaice
225 g (8 oz) fresh asparagus heads, cooked
295 g (10.4 oz) Campbell's Condensed Asparagus Soup
juice of 1 lemon
freshly ground black pepper
2 tbsp single cream or milk
Garnish: paprika

Preheat the oven, 160°C (325°F) or Gas 3. Lightly butter an ovenproof dish. Wrap each fillet round a few asparagus heads and place in the dish. Mix together the soup, lemon juice, pepper and cream and pour over the fish. Cover and cook in the oven for 30 minutes or until the fish is cooked.

Serve with new potatoes and a green salad.

[M] 5-6 minutes on high

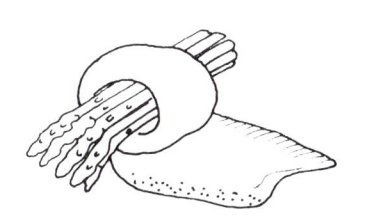

Cook's notes:

FOR WELL BEING · 105

15 *minutes*
Preparation time

**Cooking time:
5 minutes**

Serves 4

Veal or Pork Escalopes with Mushroom Sauce

Pork may easily be used in place of veal in this delicious and classic dish.

1 tbsp oil
1 onion, peeled and finely chopped
4 veal escalopes, very thinly cut (or top leg of pork may be used)
freshly ground black pepper
295 g (10.4 oz) Campbell's Condensed Cream of Mushroom Soup
juice of ½ lemon
150 ml (¼ pint) carton soured cream
Garnish: chopped parsley and lemon wedges

Heat the oil, add the onion and cook for 3 minutes. Add the meat and brown well on both sides of each escalope. Stir in remaining ingredients, cover and cook for 5 minutes over a low heat. Place on a warmed serving dish and garnish with the chopped parsley.

Serve with baby new potatoes and mange tout or broccoli.

Ⓕ   2 months

Cook's notes:

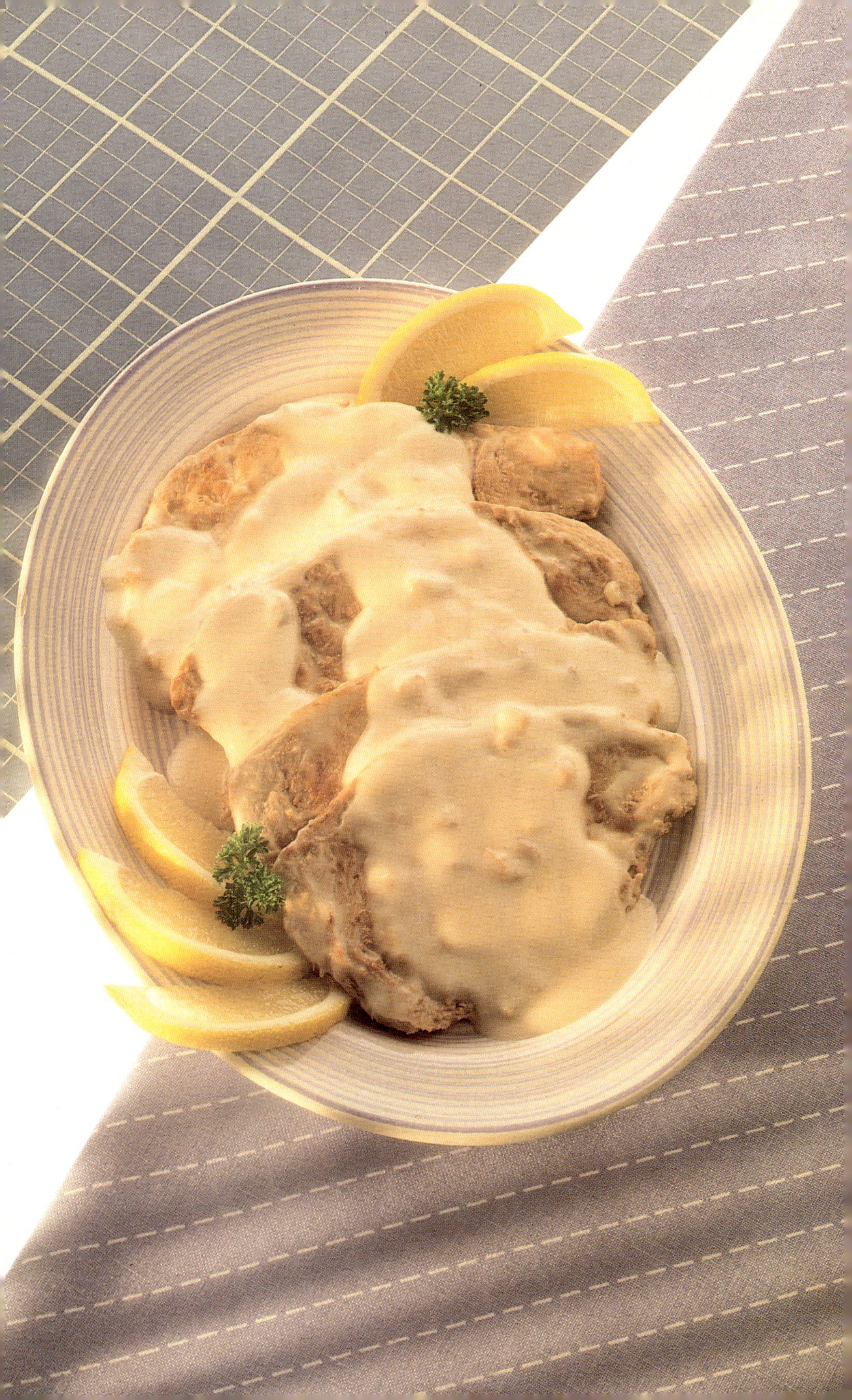

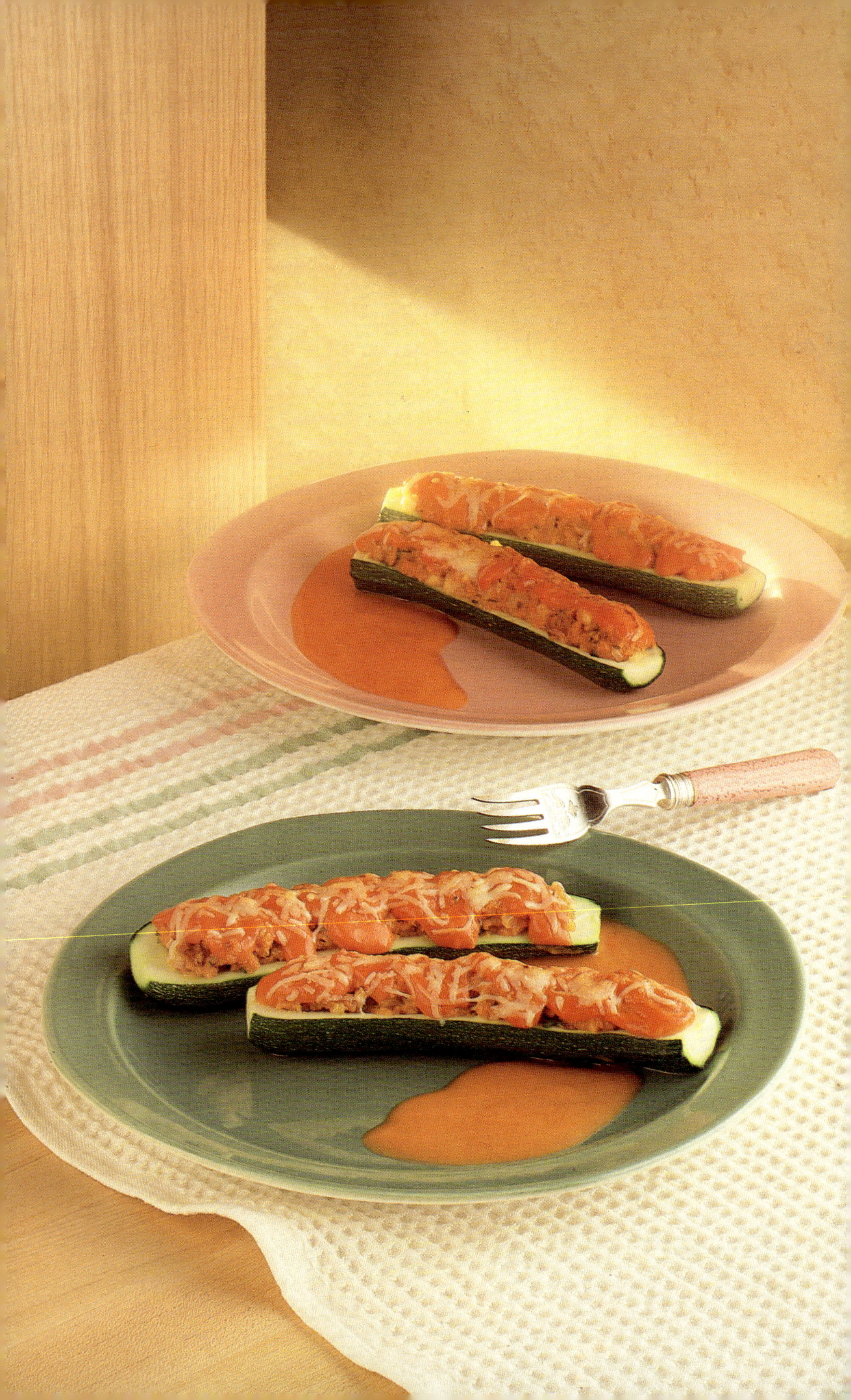

Stuffed Courgettes

This is a perfect way to prepare courgettes or marrows.

15 minutes
Preparation time

**Cooking time:
30-45 minutes**

Serves 4-6

Stuffing
a little oil
1 onion, peeled and finely chopped
50 g (2 oz) walnuts, finely chopped
1 teasp oregano
1 teasp fresh parsley, chopped
300 g (10.6 oz) Campbell's Condensed Cream of Tomato Soup
185 g (6 oz) fresh breadcrumbs
freshly ground black pepper

4-6 large courgettes or 1 medium marrow
50 g (2 oz) Cheddar cheese, grated
freshly grated nutmeg

Preheat oven, 180°C (350°F) or Gas 4. Heat oil in a pan and fry onion for 1 minute. Add rest of stuffing ingredients, using half the soup, and stir well. Cook over low heat for 5 minutes stirring occasionally. Meanwhile, cut the courgettes lengthways, scoop out the flesh and add to stuffing (if using a marrow, cut into rings and scoop out the flesh, leaving a little flesh as the base of each ring). Place the courgettes or marrow on a greased baking tray and fill with the stuffing. Mix the rest of the soup together with the cheese and nutmeg and top each courgette or marrow with the mixture. Cover and bake in the oven for 30-45 minutes or until cooked.

(F) **2 months**

Cook's notes:

15 minutes
Preparation time

Setting time:
2 hours or more

Serves 4-6

Asparagus Mousse

This is a good mousse to make quickly the day before. To make it go further you can add chopped ham or add a chopped hard-boiled egg at the last minute.

juice of 1 lemon
1 tbsp water
1 dessertsp gelatine
295 g (10.4 oz) Campbell's Condensed Asparagus Soup
150 ml (¼ pint) double cream, lightly whipped
3 eggs, separated
Garnish: bunch watercress

Put the lemon juice and water into a small saucepan and sprinkle over the gelatine. Soak and dissolve over a very low heat. Mix the soup, cream and egg yolks together in a bowl. Add the gelatine and stir well. Whisk the egg whites until very stiff and fold in, using a metal spoon. Pour into an oiled 900 ml (1½ pint) ring mould and leave to set in the fridge. To serve, turn out and garnish with watercress in the middle of the ring.

Serve with granary bread.

(F)   3 months

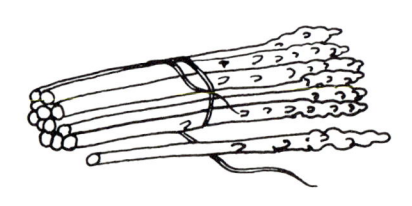

Cook's notes:

Cauliflower Cheese with Bacon

The perfect meal after a hard day. It is very quick to prepare and to cook; it tastes delicious with the sizzling bacon surrounding the cauliflower and it has the added bonus of being low in calories.

15 minutes Preparation time

Cooking time: 15 minutes

Serves 4

1 medium cauliflower, cut into four
8 rashers streaky bacon, rinds removed
295 g (10.4 oz) Campbell's Condensed Cream of Celery Soup
juice of 1/2 lemon
salt and freshly ground black pepper
150 ml (1/4 pint) natural yoghurt
50 g (2 oz) Cheddar cheese, grated

Cook the cauliflower in boiling salted water for about 10 minutes or until it is turning soft but still holding its shape. Grill or fry the bacon until crispy. Meanwhile mix the soup, salt and pepper, lemon juice and yoghurt in a saucepan and heat gently. Arrange the cauliflower in a warmed serving dish, place the bacon round the sides and pour over the sauce. Top with the cheese and brown under a preheated hot grill. Serve immediately.

Serve with a tomato and onion salad.

Cook's notes:

20 minutes
Preparation time

Cooking time:
45 minutes-1 hour

Serves 6

Saucy Stuffed Aubergines

This is a very good dish to serve vegetarians and also makes an excellent supper dish with the added goodness and flavour of the nuts and cheese.

3 medium aubergines
salt and freshly ground black pepper
4 tbsp oil
1 clove garlic, peeled and crushed
1 onion, peeled and finely chopped
300 g (10.6 oz) Campbell's Condensed Tomato and Rice Soup
1 teasp oregano
1 tbsp walnuts, finely chopped
50 g (2 oz) Cheddar cheese, grated

Preheat the oven, 180°C (350°F) or Gas 4. Cut aubergines in half lengthways, scoop out the flesh and sprinkle with salt to extract the bitter juices. Leave for 5 minutes. Meanwhile, heat the oil in a saucepan and add the garlic and onion. Fry for 3 minutes. Add the soup, oregano and walnuts. Wipe and dry the aubergine flesh and chop finely. Add to the soup mixture and cook for 3 minutes. Fill the aubergine skins, top with the grated cheese, place in an ovenproof dish and cook for about 45 minutes or until the skins are soft.

[M] 8 minutes on high

Cook's notes:

Rabbit in Mustard Sauce

Rabbit is an increasingly popular meat. It is very cheap, has very little fat or waste and, cooked in this sauce, it is perfect for any occasion.

15 minutes Preparation time

Cooking time: 1 hour

Serves 4

4 rashers bacon, rind removed and chopped
a little oil
1 onion, peeled and finely chopped
1 clove garlic, peeled and crushed
4 medium-sized rabbit joints
295 g (10.4 oz) Campbell's Condensed Cream of Chicken Soup
1 dessertsp seed mustard
4 tbsp white wine
Garnish: parsley, chopped

Preheat the oven, 180°C (350°F) or Gas 4. Heat the oil in a large casserole, add the bacon, onion and garlic and cook for 3 minutes. Add the remaining ingredients. Stir well, cover and cook for 1 hour in the oven. Garnish with the parsley and serve.

Serve with new potatoes and a green vegetable.

Cook's notes:

15 *minutes*
Preparation time

Cooking time:
25 minutes

Serves 4-6

Okra Ratatouille and Cheese

Use courgettes or okra. The other word for okra is lady's fingers, often used in Indian cookery. Try to find young, tender okra.

2 tbsp oil
2 cloves garlic, peeled and crushed
1 large onion, peeled and finely chopped
2 aubergines, wiped and sliced
225 g (8 oz) okra or courgettes
1 green pepper, cored and chopped
salt and freshly ground black pepper
295 g (10.4 oz) Campbell's Condensed Vegetable Soup
1 teasp tomato puree
50 g (2 oz) Cheddar cheese, grated

Heat the oil in a large pan and add the garlic and onion. Cook for 3 minutes and then add all remaining ingredients, except the cheese, and stir well. Cover and simmer on a very low heat for 20 minutes. Place in a warmed serving dish and sprinkle over the cheese. Brown quickly under a hot grill and serve.

(F) 2 months

[M] 6 minutes on high

Cook's notes:

Prawns in Plaice

This dish is low in calories and full of healthy goodies. It is extremely versatile – the perfect supper dish or just as good served as the main course at a smart dinner party.

15 minutes Preparation time

Cooking time: 30 minutes

Serves 4

295 g (10.4 oz) Campbell's Condensed Cream of Mushroom Soup
juice of ½ lemon
a dash of Tabasco
1 tbsp white wine
freshly ground black pepper
125 g (4 oz) peeled prawns, thawed
pinch basil
4 fillets of plaice
a knob of butter
150 ml (¼ pint) natural yoghurt
1 dessertsp chopped parsley
Garnish: 4 unshelled large prawns, a few fresh basil leaves

Preheat the oven, 180°C (350°F) or Gas 4. In a saucepan, heat the soup, lemon juice, Tabasco, white wine and black pepper, stirring well. Adjust seasoning to taste. Halve the mixture and to one half add the prawns and the basil. Stir well. Lay out the fillets and spoon the prawn and soup mixture onto each fillet. Roll up and lay in a buttered ovenproof dish. Add the yoghurt and parsley to the rest of the soup mixture and spoon over the fish. Cover the dish and bake in the oven for about 30 minutes or until the fish is cooked through. Garnish with whole prawns and fresh basil and serve.

Serve with brown rice and a tomato salad.

(F) 1 month

Cook's notes:

5 *minutes*
Preparation time

Soaking time:
1 hour

Cooking time:
15 minutes

Serves 4

Sweetbreads with Chicken Sauce

Sweetbreads have one of the most delicate flavours of all meats. They are very simple to cook and are full of goodness.

450 g (1 lb) sweetbreads
295 g (10.4 oz) Campbell's Condensed Cream of Chicken Soup
1 tbsp parsley, finely chopped
salt and freshly ground black pepper

Soak the sweetbreads in salted water for about 1 hour. Rinse and remove any stringy bits. Place in boiling salted water and simmer for 15 minutes. Meanwhile, heat the soup in a saucepan and add the parsley and pepper. Drain the sweetbreads and add to the soup. Stir well and serve.

Serve with brown rice and a green vegetable.

Cook's notes:

Squid in Crab Sauce

Squid are delicious and the preparation is fun and not difficult. Simply wash them well under running water to rinse out the black 'ink' then remove the thin outer skin with its black markings. Draw out the backbone and slice into rings.

25 minutes
Preparation time

Cooking time:
5 minutes

Serves 4

1 tbsp oil
1 onion, peeled and finely chopped
1 clove garlic, peeled and crushed
450 g (1 lb) squid, washed, prepared and drained
freshly ground black pepper
295 g (10.4 oz) Campbell's Condensed Crab Bisque
1 tbsp chopped parsley
juice of ½ lemon
a few drops of Tabasco
150 ml (¼ pint) soured cream
Garnish: 1 lemon cut into wedges

Heat the oil in a frying pan. Add the onion and garlic and cook for 3 minutes. Add the squid and cook for a further 5 minutes. Add the pepper, soup, parsley, lemon juice, Tabasco and white wine and mix together well. Cover and simmer for 5 minutes. Stir in the soured cream and arrange on a warmed serving dish. Garnish with lemon wedges.

Serve with brown rice and a mixed salad.

(F)   1 month

Cook's notes:

15 minutes
Preparation time

Cooking time:
1 hour

Serves 3-4

Chicken with Grapes

Cooked in a wine-flavoured sauce, chicken and grapes make a delicious combination.

a little oil
1 onion, peeled and finely chopped
1 chicken, jointed
salt and freshly ground black pepper
225 g (8 oz) white seedless grapes, off the stalk
juice of ½ lemon
4 tbsp white wine
295 g (10.4 oz) Campbell's Condensed Cream of Celery Soup
Garnish: a few grapes and lemon wedges

Preheat the oven, 180°C (350°F) or Gas 4. Heat oil in a casserole, add onion and fry for 3 minutes. Add chicken joints and brown slightly on all sides. Add all remaining ingredients. Cover and cook for 1 hour. Garnish with grapes and lemon wedges and serve.

Serve with new potatoes and broccoli.

(F)   3 months (omit grapes)

[M]   8 minutes on high and 10 minutes standing time

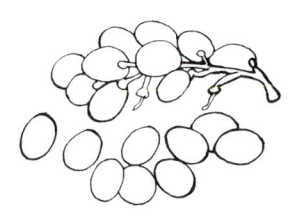

Cook's notes:

FOR PARTIES

Campbell's Condensed can help you to make light of entertaining. If you want to impress your guests and enjoy the party you will find our recipes the perfect shortcut.

15 minutes
Preparation time

**Cooking time:
20 minutes**

Serves 4

Pork Chops with Orange and Apple

This is an old favourite at home and has always proved a great success. So quick and easy and yet looks very impressive.

a little oil
4 pork chops, rind removed and fat trimmed
1 orange, sliced
1 apple, sliced
8 whole cloves
295 g (10.4 oz) Campbell's Condensed Consomme
1 dessertsp brown sugar
a little cinnamon
1 dessertsp cornflour
2 tbsp orange juice

Brown the chops in the oil in a large frying pan. Place a slice of orange then apple on each chop and secure with two cloves. Add the consomme, sugar and cinnamon. Cover and cook over a low heat for 20 minutes or until the chops are cooked. Mix the cornflour and orange juice in a cup. Put the chops onto a warmed serving dish. Add the cornflour mixture to the juices and stir continuously over a low heat until thickened. Pour over the chops and serve.

Serve with mashed potatoes and petit pois.

(F)   2 months

Cook's notes:

Gingered Up Lamb Chops

A delicious casserole of lamb chops cooked with fresh rosemary and wine and spiked with fresh ginger.

295 g (10.4 oz) Campbell's Condensed Vegetable Soup
3 tbsp red wine
1 teasp freshly chopped rosemary
chunk of fresh root ginger, peeled and coarsely grated
4 loin lamb chops
Garnish: few sprigs of rosemary

Preheat the oven, 180°C (350°F) or Gas 4. Combine all the ingredients, except the chops, to make a sauce. Place the chops in a casserole dish, stir the sauce well and pour over the chops. Cover. Cook in the oven for about 1 hour or until the chops are tender. Test for seasoning and then serve.

Serve with new potatoes and crunchy green beans.

(F)   2 months

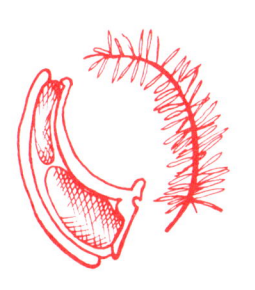

10 *minutes*
Preparation time

Cooking time:
1 hour

Serves 2

Cook's notes:

15 *minutes*
Preparation time

Cooking time:
40 minutes

Serves 4

Honey Duck with Orange

Duck is too fatty to cook in a casserole so this is the perfect answer and the tasty juices from the bottom of the pan can be made into a fruity sauce.

4 duck portions
a little honey
295 g (10.4 oz) Campbell's Condensed Consomme
juice of 2 oranges
juice of 1 lemon
1 dessertsp brown sugar
1 tbsp port
1 dessertsp cornflour
Garnish: 1 sliced orange, 1 bunch watercress

Preheat the oven, 200°C (400°F) or Gas 6. Prick duck all over with a fork and dry the skin. Using your hands, rub the honey on the duck skin, place on a wire rack over a baking tin and cook for 40 minutes or until crispy and golden. Meanwhile, heat the consomme, fruit juices and brown sugar together. Mix the port and cornflour in a cup. When the duck is cooked, pour off all the fat and add the remaining juices to the consomme. Add the cornflour mixture and stir continuously over a very low heat until the sauce thickens. Arrange the duck portions on a warmed serving dish and spoon over the sauce. Garnish with the orange slices and watercress.

Serve with new potatoes and petit pois.

(F) 2 months

Cook's notes:

Chicken Divan

Slices of mango tucked inside chicken breasts add an exotic flavour to this dish and the coating of mushroom sauce wraps it up to perfection.

15 minutes Preparation time

Cooking time: 30 minutes

Serves 4

4 chicken breasts
1 small mango or peach, peeled and sliced
450 g (1 lb) broccoli, cooked
295 g (10.4 oz) Campbell's Condensed Cream of Mushroom Soup
1 tbsp sherry
1 teasp Worcestershire sauce
freshly ground black pepper
150 ml ($1/4$ pint) cream
Garnish: watercress

Preheat the oven, 180°C (350°F) or Gas 4. Stuff the chicken breasts with the slices of mango. Lay the broccoli over the bottom of an ovenproof dish. Lay the chicken breasts on top. Mix the remaining ingredients together and pour over the chicken. Cook in the oven for 30 minutes or until the breasts are cooked. Garnish with watercress and serve.

Serve with new potatoes and glazed carrots.

(F) 2 months

[M] 8 minutes on high and 10 minutes standing time

Cook's notes:

20 minutes
Preparation time

Cooking time:
30 minutes

Serves 4-6

Spinach Roulade with Mushrooms

If you use Campbell's Condensed Cream of Mushroom Soup then this recipe could not be easier. No more white sauces to make and the consistency is always perfect.

450 g (1 lb) spinach, washed and destalked
salt and freshly ground black pepper
a little fresh nutmeg
4 eggs, separated
295 g (10.4 oz) Campbell's Condensed Cream of Mushroom Soup
juice of ½ lemon
grated Parmesan cheese

Preheat the oven, 180°C (350°F) or Gas 4. Cook the spinach in boiling salted water for 10 minutes, drain and squeeze out very well. Chop finely and mix with half the mushroom soup, nutmeg, pepper and egg yolks. Whisk the egg whites until stiff and fold in with a metal spoon. Pour into a Swiss roll tin 33 cm (13 inches) by 23 cm (9 inches) lined with greaseproof paper. Cook in the oven for 20 minutes or until the mixture is firm but not browning. Meanwhile, mix the rest of the mushroom soup with the lemon juice. When spinach is cool spread over the mushroom mixture and roll up lengthways, carefully removing greaseproof paper as you roll. Place on a plate and sprinkle with Parmesan.

If presented as a starter, serve with bread and butter.

If presented as a main course, serve with a green salad.

(F)   2 months

Cook's notes:

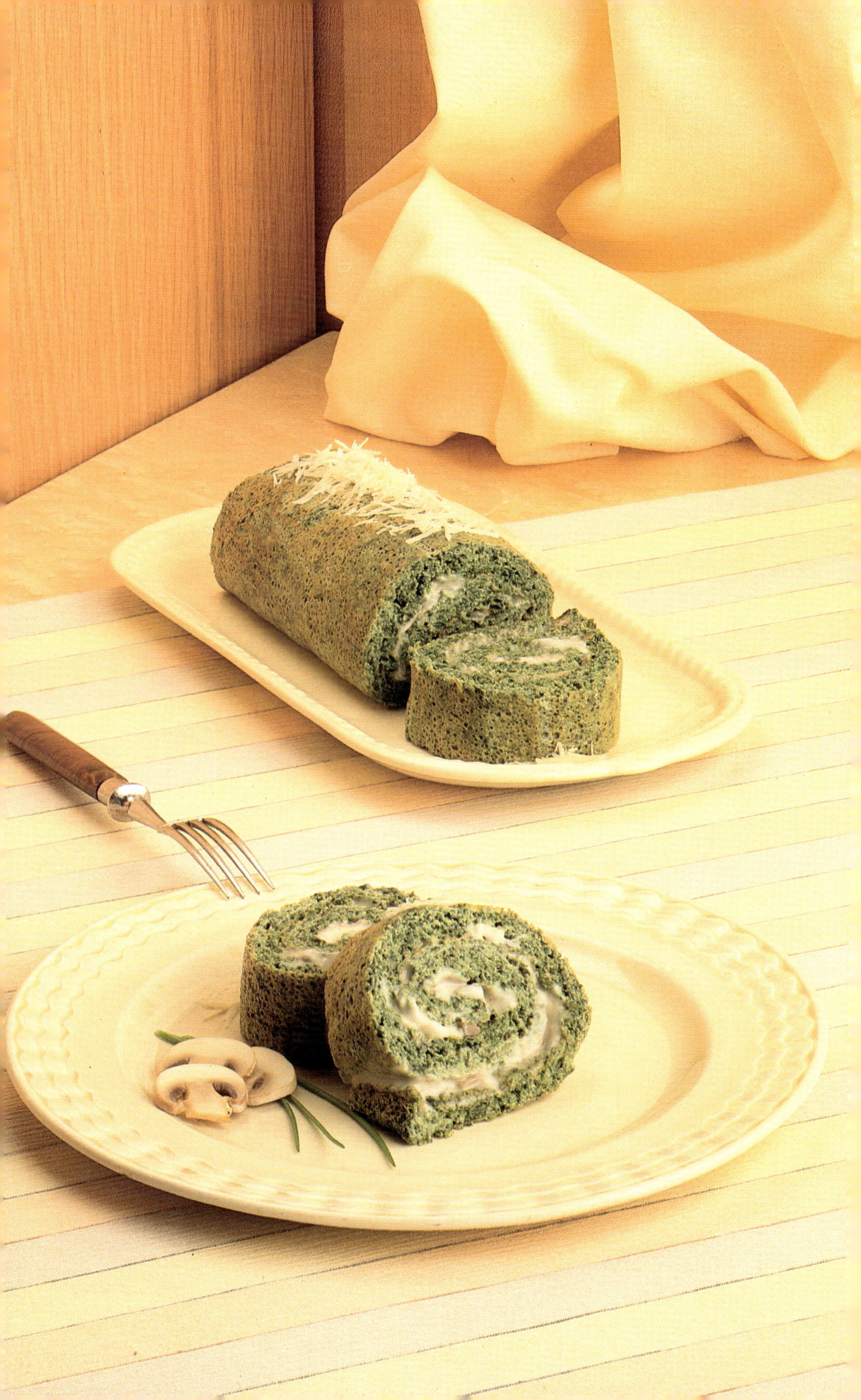

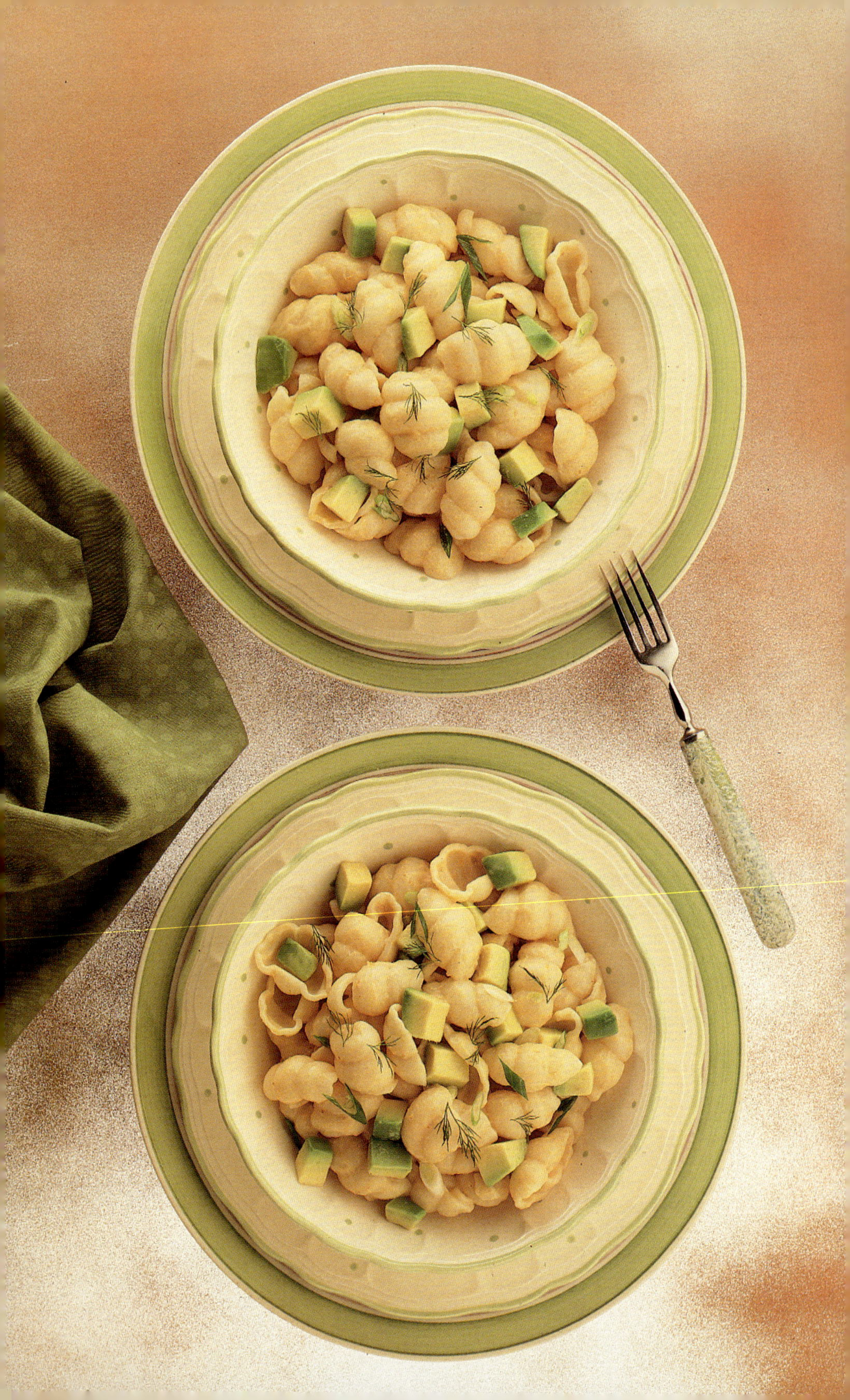

Smoked Salmon and Avocado Pasta

A very quick, light and easy dish, perfect for a summer's day.

10 minutes
Preparation time

**Cooking time:
10 minutes**

Serves 4-6

450 g (1 lb) pasta shells
295 g (10.4 oz) Campbell's Condensed Cream of Smoked Salmon Soup
a little water
2 avocados
juice of ½ lemon
6 spring onions, chopped
lots of freshly ground black pepper
salt
Garnish: fresh dill or parsley and lemon

Cook the pasta in boiling salted water for 10 minutes or until just tender. Drain and rinse under cold water. Mix with the soup and a little water. Cut the avocados in half and remove stones. Cut the flesh into squares without damaging the skin. Scoop out and add to the pasta dish. Add the lemon juice, spring onions and pepper and stir carefully.

Serve with herb or garlic bread.

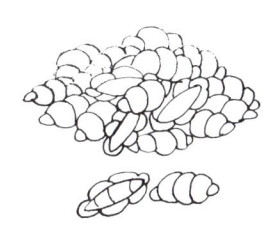

Cook's notes:

15 *minutes*
Preparation time

Setting time:
2 hours

Serves 4-6

Chicken and Ham Mousse

Very good for a party as it can be made the day before and turned out just before your guests arrive.

3 eggs, separated
295 g (10.4 oz) Campbell's Condensed Chicken Soup
50 g (2 oz) ham, cooked and chopped
freshly ground black pepper
a little tarragon
150 ml ($1/4$ pint) soured cream
juice of 1 lemon
1 dessertsp gelatine
Garnish: 1 lemon sliced, 1 bunch watercress

Mix the egg yolks, soup, ham, pepper, tarragon and soured cream together. Put the lemon juice in a small saucepan and sprinkle over the gelatine. Soak and then dissolve over a low heat. Stir into the soup mixture. Whisk the egg whites until stiff and fold into the mixture with a metal spoon. Pour into an oiled 600 ml (1 pint) soufflé dish or mould and chill until set. Turn out onto a serving dish and garnish with the lemon slices and watercress.

Serve with brown bread and butter.

Ⓕ   **2 months**

Cook's notes:

Beef Olives with Cream Cheese

This makes a lovely change from the typical breadcrumb stuffing and is much more succulent and creamy. If you can't buy such a small amount of sausage meat, just peel the skins off some ordinary sausages.

15 minutes
Preparation time

Cooking time:
1½ hours

Serves 8

a little oil
1 onion, peeled and chopped finely
125 g (4 oz) cream cheese
125 g (4 oz) sausage meat
1 tbsp parsley, chopped
freshly ground black pepper
1 teasp thyme
juice of ½ lemon
450 g (1 lb) topside beef, sliced very thinly
300 g (10.6 oz) Campbell's Condensed Cream of Tomato Soup
1 teasp Worcestershire sauce
1 teasp basil

Preheat the oven, 180°C (350°F) or Gas 4. Heat the oil in a pan, add the onion and fry for 3 minutes. Mix the cheese, sausage meat, parsley, pepper, thyme and lemon juice together in a bowl, add the onion and mix well again. Spread on the slices of beef and roll up, securing with a cocktail stick if necessary. Put into an ovenproof dish, mix the soup with the Worcestershire sauce and basil and pour over the beef olives. Cover and cook in the oven for 1½ hours or until the meat is really tender.

Served with mashed potatoes and green beans.

Ⓕ   **3 months**

Cook's notes:

15 minutes
Preparation time

Cooking time:
2 hours 20 minutes

Serves 6

Steak, Kidney and Ale Pie

The addition of a can of smoked oysters makes this a very glamorous dinner dish for the winter. Smoked oysters are available at most supermarkets and are surprisingly inexpensive.

450 g (1 lb) stewing steak, cubed
225 g (8 oz) ox kidney, chopped
295 g (10.4 oz) Campbell's Condensed French Onion Soup
freshly ground black pepper
150 ml (¼ pint) brown ale or water
1 can smoked oysters (optional)
225 g (8 oz) packet shortcrust pastry
milk for glaze

Preheat the oven, 200°C (400°F) or Gas 6. Mix the meat, soup and pepper together and then stir in the ale or water. Pour into a 1 litre (2 pint) pie dish. Lay the smoked oysters over the top. Roll out the pastry, wet the edges of the dish and then lay over. Trim the edges and press down with a fork. Glaze with the milk and cook for 20 minutes or until golden and then reduce the oven temperature to 150°C (300°F) or Gas 2 for 2 hours.

Serve with mashed potatoes and Brussels sprouts with chestnuts.

Ⓕ   3 months

Cook's notes:

Cider Pork with Fruit

A lovely fresh and fruity-flavoured sauce made extra special by adding Calvados. This is a delightful dish all the year round.

15 minutes
Preparation time

Cooking time: 20 minutes

Serves 4

a little oil
1 onion, peeled and chopped finely
6 pork chops
1 dessert apple, peeled, cored and chopped
295 g (10.4 oz) Campbell's Condensed Cream of Celery Soup
freshly ground black pepper
150 ml (¼ pint) cider
1 tbsp Calvados (optional)
Garnish: celery tops or parsley, chopped

Heat the oil in a large frying pan, add the onion and fry for 3 minutes. Add the chops and brown on both sides and then strain off the fat. Add all the other ingredients, stir well. Cover and cook for 20 minutes on a low heat or until the chops are cooked. Place on a warmed serving dish and garnish.

Serve with new potatoes and glazed carrots.

Ⓕ   **2 months**

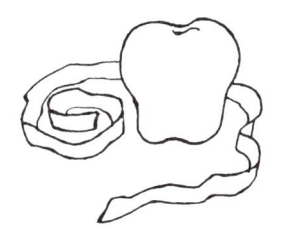

Cook's notes:

15 *minutes*
Preparation time

Cooking time:
1 hour

Serves 3-4

Pheasant in Brandy

One of the best flavoured game birds in this country, it only needs the addition of a very mild and subtle sauce.

a little oil
1 pheasant
295 g (10.4 oz) Campbell's Condensed French Onion Soup
50 g (2 oz) button mushrooms, wiped and sliced
125 g (4 oz) seedless grapes
freshly ground black pepper
1 tbsp brandy
4 tbsp single cream
1 tbsp parsley, chopped
Garnish: a few grapes and sprigs of parsley

Preheat the oven, 160°C (325°F) or Gas 3. Heat the oil in a casserole and brown the bird on all sides. Add the soup, mushrooms, grapes and pepper. Stir well, cover and cook for 1 hour in the oven. Add the brandy, cream and parsley to the sauce. Joint the bird, arrange the pieces on a warmed serving dish and then spoon over the sauce. Garnish with the grapes and parsley.

Serve with French-style chips or crisps and broccoli.

(F)   3 months

Cook's notes:

Lamb Chops with Barbecue Sauce

This is a wonderful sauce for chops, spare ribs or even chicken drumsticks – it takes only seconds to prepare. If the meat is very fatty then fry quickly first to remove some of the fat.

**10 minutes
Preparation time**

**Cooking time:
45 minutes**

Serves 4

1 tbsp dark brown sugar
1 teasp dried mustard
1 tbsp vinegar
½ teasp paprika
1 tbsp Worcestershire sauce
1 tbsp lemon juice
1 tbsp runny honey
300 g (10.6 oz) Campbell's Condensed Cream of Tomato Soup
8 lean lamb chops
Garnish: slices of fresh tomato and parsley

Put all the ingredients except the chops into a bowl and mix well. Place the chops in an ovenproof dish and pour over the sauce. Rub well into the meat and then leave for one hour. Preheat the oven, 200°C (400°F) or Gas 6. Place in the middle of the oven and cook for about 45 minutes or until the chops are glossy and crispy. Garnish with slices of fresh tomato and parsley and serve.

Serve with saffron or tumeric rice and a crispy green salad.

(F)   2 months

Cook's notes:

15 minutes
Preparation time

Cooking time:
1-1½ hours

Serves 4

Beef Carbonnade

Beef cooked in beer gives a lovely nutty flavour and this recipe also has a super topping of mustard-encrusted French bread.

a little oil
2 onions, peeled and sliced
2 cloves garlic, peeled and crushed
900 g (2 lb) chuck steak, cut into cubes
1 tbsp soft brown sugar
295 g (10.4 oz) Campbell's Condensed Oxtail Soup
300 ml (½ pint) stout or brown ale
1 bouquet garni
2 bay leaves
slices of French bread
Dijon mustard

Preheat the oven, 160°C (325°F) or Gas 3. Heat oil in the casserole, add onions and garlic and fry for 3 minutes. Add the meat and brown slightly. Add all remaining ingredients and stir well. Cover and cook for 1-1½ hours or until the meat is tender. Approximately 20-30 minutes before the casserole is cooked you might like to add an extra touch. Spread the Dijon mustard on one side of the slices of French bread. Arrange the slices on top of the casserole mustard-side up. Use the back of a spoon to submerge the bread. The bread will magically rise to the surface again and become crispy on top. Delicious! Remove the bouquet garni and bay leaves and serve.

Serve with small baked potatoes and Brussels sprouts with chestnuts.

(F)   3 months

Cook's notes:

Chicken and Asparagus Casserole

Asparagus has a lovely mellow flavour and spiked with a little lemon juice is a perfect complement to chicken.

15 minutes Preparation time

Cooking time: 1 hour

Serves 4

4 rashers streaky bacon, chopped
a little oil
1 onion, peeled and chopped
4 chicken joints
295 g (10.4 oz) Campbell's Condensed Asparagus Soup
juice of ½ lemon
4 tbsp milk
freshly ground black pepper
2 courgettes, wiped and sliced

Preheat the oven, 180°C (350°F) or Gas 4. Put the bacon and oil in the casserole and add the onion. Fry for 3 minutes. Add the chicken joints and brown on both sides. Add remaining ingredients and mix well. Cover and cook in the oven for 1 hour or until the chicken is tender.

Serve with boiled new potatoes and green vegetables.

(F) 3 months

[M] 8 minutes on high and 10 minutes standing time

Cook's notes:

20 minutes
Preparation time

**Cooking time:
20 minutes**

Serves 4-6

Crab and Egg Roulade

This is an extra smart roulade with the well married flavours of crab and hard-boiled egg. Very easy to make so don't be afraid.

295 g (10.4 oz) Campbell's Condensed Crab Bisque
a dash of Tabasco
juice of 1/2 lemon
lots of freshly ground black pepper
1 tbsp parsley
4 eggs, separated
295 g (10.4 oz) Campbell's Condensed Cream of Celery Soup
2 hard-boiled eggs, shelled and chopped
more pepper

Preheat the oven, 180°C (350°F) or Gas 4. Line a 33 cm (13 inch) by 23 cm (9 inch) Swiss roll tin with greaseproof paper. Mix the crab soup, Tabasco, lemon juice, pepper and parsley together. Add the egg yolks. Whisk the egg whites until stiff and then fold in using a metal spoon. Pour into the prepared tin and cook in the oven for 20 minutes or until set but not browning. Meanwhile, mix the celery soup with the hard-boiled eggs and pepper and spread over the cooled crab mixture. Roll up lengthways, carefully removing the greaseproof paper as you roll. Place on a plate and serve in slices.

Serve with bread and butter.

Cook's notes:

Mushroom Tartlets

The only part of this recipe that takes time is making the pastry shells. I advise you to make a large batch and freeze those you don't need or keep them in an airtight tin for up to a week.

15 minutes
Preparation time

Cooking time:
10 minutes

Serves 4

1 × 225 g (8 oz) packet shortcrust pastry
1 tbsp flour and grated Parmesan cheese mixed together
295 g (10.4 oz) Campbell's Condensed Cream of Mushroom Soup
1 tbsp sherry
1 teasp freshly chopped parsley
1 tbsp soured cream, yoghurt or double cream
Garnish: sprigs of parsley

Preheat the oven, 180°C (350°F) or Gas 4. Roll out the pastry on a board sprinkled with the flour and cheese mixture and using a 7 cm (3 inch) circular pastry cutter press out at least 8 shapes and place them in tartlet tins. (Make smaller tartlets to serve with drinks.) Cover and press down with small pieces of foil and bake in the oven for about 10 minutes or until slightly crispy and pale brown. While the pastry is cooking empty the soup into a saucepan and add the remaining ingredients. Heat gently and stir well. Spoon the warm sauce into the pastry cases, garnish with the parsley and serve immediately.

(F) **2 months for pastry shells**

1 month for mushroom sauce

Cook's notes:

15 minutes Preparation time

Dips

Dips are a very good cocktail accompaniment, particularly with lovely brightly coloured vegetables served around each bowl. They are also good if you have friends to dinner and don't want to serve a starter at the table.

Blue Cheese Dip
225 g (8 oz) Gorgonzola or Dolcelatte cheese, rind removed
295 g (10.4 oz) Campbell's Condensed Cream of Celery Soup
juice of ½ lemon
freshly ground black pepper
few sprigs parsley

Put all the ingredients in a blender and turn to high for 1 minute or until smooth. Put into a bowl and serve with crisps and crudités.

Curried Chicken Dip
295 g (10.4 oz) Campbell's Condensed Cream of Chicken Soup
2 hard-boiled eggs, shelled and chopped roughly
1 tomato, skinned
juice of ½ lemon
freshly ground black pepper
¼ teasp curry powder
1 teasp mango chutney

Put all the ingredients in a blender and turn to high for 1 minute or until smooth. Put into serving bowl and serve with crisps and crudités.

For Crudités
Use carrots, radishes, celery, cauliflower, chicory, cucumber, raw mushrooms, courgettes and cabbage slices all washed and cut into edible-sized pieces.

Cook's notes:

INDEX

Anchovy and Onion Tart, 11
Asparagus Loaves, 13
Asparagus Mousse, 110
Avocado
   Hot Avocado with Crab, 7

Baked Potatoes with various fillings, 39
Beef
   Beef Bourguignon, 83
   Beef Carbonnade, 134
   Beef Goulash, 63
   Beefy Meat Loaf, 54
   Beef Olives with Cream Cheese, 129
   Beef Strogonoff, 91
   Braised Brisket of Beef, 61
   Chocolate Chilli Con Carne, 96
   Munchy Meatballs, 64
   Spicy Hamburgers, 35
   Steak, Kidney and Ale Pie, 130
Bobotie, 94
Bouillabaisse, 32

Cartwheel Soup, 30
Catalonian Bread, 40
Canton Fish Dish, 88
Cassoulet, 84
Cauliflower Cheese with Bacon, 111
Cheese and Celery Scones, 37
Chicken
   Chicken and Asparagus Casserole, 135
   Chicken and Bacon Flan, 57
   Chicken and Bacon Soufflé, 101
   Chicken and Banana Pie, 50
   Chicken Casserole with Peanuts, 95
   Chicken Curry, 97
   Chicken Divan, 123
   Chicken with Grapes, 118
   Chicken and Ham Mousse, 128
   Macaroni Chicken, 46
   Paella, 82
Chicory and Ham Beds, 41
Chilled Consomme, 10
Chocolate Chilli Con Carne, 96
Cider Pork with Fruit, 131
Consommed Eggs, 22
Cottage Pie, 68
Crab and Cheese Soufflé, 102
Crab and Egg Roulade, 136
Crab in Seashells, 14
Cream Ham Mousse, 20
Crowned Snaffles Mousse, 9
Curried Sweetcorn Soup, 28

Devilled Grilled Eggs, 42
Duck
   Honey Duck with Orange, 122
Dips, 138

Eggs
   Consommed Eggs, 22
   Crab and Egg Roulade, 136
   Devilled Grilled Eggs, 42
   Prawn and Egg Curry, 98
   Scrambled Egg with Chicken, 47
   Spinach Bed for Eggs, 48
   Spinach Roulade with Mushrooms, 124
   Stuffed Eggs with Asparagus, 21

Fish
   Bouillabaisse, 32
   Canton Fish Dish, 88
   Crab and Egg Roulade, 136
   Crab and Cheese Soufflé, 102
   Fish Pasties, 56
   Fish Pie, 66
   Floating Crab Soup, 29
   Layered Fish Terrine, 23-24
   Moules Provençales, 103
   Plaice with Asparagus, 105
   Prawn and Cheese Pâté, 36
   Prawn and Egg Curry, 98
   Prawn and Herb Mousse, 18
   Prawns in Plaice, 115
   Salmon and Asparagus Quiche, 58
   Scotch Salmon with Prawn Sauce, 76
   Seafood Lasagne, 78
   Seafood Shells, 19
   Seafood Tart, 45
   Smoked Mackerel Pâté, 31
   Smoked Salmon and Avocado Pasta, 127
   Smoked Salmon Mousse in Lemon Shells, 12
   Spaghetti with Tuna, 62
   Squid in Crab Sauce, 117
   Sweet and Sour Prawns, 87
   Tuna Florentine, 44

Gingered Up Lamb Chops, 121
Gnocchi, 81

Ham
   Chicken and Ham Mousse, 128
   Chicory and Ham Beds, 41
   Cream Ham Mousse, 20
Hamburgers
   Spicy Hamburgers, 35
Honey Duck with Orange, 122
Hot Avocado with Crab, 7

Lamb
   Gingered Up Lamb Chops, 121
   Lamb Chops with Barbecue Sauce, 133
   Lamb Kebabs with Orange and Spiced Rice, 86
   Lamb's Liver Pâté, 8

Navarin of Lamb, 53
Layered Fish Terrine, 23-24
Layered Potatoes with Consomme, 75
Liver
   Oriental Calf's Liver, 65

Macaroni Chicken, 46
Moussaka, 85
Moules Provençales, 103
Munchy Meatballs, 64
Mushrooms
   Mushrooms à la Greque, 104
   Mushroom Tartlets, 137
   Spinach Roulade with Mushrooms, 124
   Stuffed Mushrooms, 6

Navarin of Lamb, 53

Okra Ratatouille and Cheese, 114
Oriental Calf's Liver, 65
Osso Bucco, 80

Paella, 82
Pancakes
   Stuffed Pancakes, 73-74
Pasta
   Macaroni Chicken, 46
   Salami Cannelloni, 79
   Seafood Lasagne, 78
   Smoked Salmon and Avocado Pasta, 127
   Spaghetti with Tuna, 62
Pâté
   Lamb's Liver Pâté, 8
   Prawn and Cheese Pâté, 36
   Smoked Mackerel Pâté, 31
Pheasant in Brandy, 132
Pizza Baps, 43
Plaice with Asparagus, 105
Pork
   Cider Pork with Fruit, 131
   Pork Chops with Orange and Apple, 120
   Pork or Veal Escalopes with Mushroom Sauce, 106
   Pork and Haricot Casserole, 67
   Pork Paprika, 92
   Porky Pea Soup, 26
   Porky Pie, 59
Potatoes
   Baked Potatoes with various fillings, 39
Prawns
   Prawn and Cheese Pâté, 36
   Prawn and Egg Curry, 98
   Prawn and Herb Mousse, 18
   Prawns in Plaice, 115
   Sweet and Sour Prawns, 87

Rabbit in Mustard Sauce, 113
Ratatouille
   Okra Ratatouille and Cheese, 114

Salami Cannelloni, 79
Salmon and Asparagus Quiche, 58
Saucy Stuffed Aubergines, 112
Sausage and Kidney Sauté, 55
Scotch Salmon with Prawn Sauce, 76
Scrambled Egg with Chicken, 47
Seafood Lasagne, 78
Seafood Shells, 19
Seafood Tart, 45
Smoked Mackerel Pâté, 31
Smoked Salmon and Avocado Pasta, 127
Smoked Salmon Mousse in Lemon
   Shells, 12
Soup
   Bouillabaisse, 32
   Cartwheel Soup, 30
   Curried Sweetcorn Soup, 28
   Floating Crab Soup, 29
   Porky Pea Soup, 26
   Vichyssoise, 27
Spaghetti with Tuna, 62
Spicy Hamburgers, 35
Spinach Bed for Eggs, 48
Spinach Roulade with Mushrooms, 124
Squid in Crab Sauce, 117
Steak, Kidney and Ale Pie, 130
Stuffed Courgettes, 109
Stuffed Eggs with Asparagus, 21
Stuffed Mushrooms, 6
Stuffed Onions, 100
Stuffed Pancakes, 73-74
Sweetbreads with Chicken Sauce, 116
Sweet and Sour Prawns, 87

Tomato Moulds with Herb Sauce, 17
Tuna Florentine, 44
Turkey Risotto, 60

Veal or Pork Escalopes with Mushroom Sauce, 106
Vegetables
   Asparagus Mousse, 110
   Baked Potatoes with various fillings, 39
   Cauliflower Cheese with Bacon, 111
   Layered Potatoes with Consommé, 75
   Mushrooms à la Greque, 104
   Mushroom Tartlets, 137
   Okra Ratatouille and Cheese, 114
   Spinach Bed for Eggs, 48
   Spinach Roulade with Mushrooms, 123
   Saucy Stuffed Aubergines, 112
   Stuffed Courgettes, 109
   Stuffed Mushrooms, 6
   Stuffed Onions, 100
Vichyssoise, 27
Vol au Vents, 38

West Indian Risotto, 93